Bessie Wheeler Gay

Her Story

Donna Gay D'Addario

Bessie Wheeler Gay: Her Story

Copyright ©2016 by Donna Gay D'Addario

ISBN-13: 978-1537302874

ISBN-10: 1537302876

Table of Contents

Cover Portrait: Bessie Maude Wheeler at 14 years

Dedication

This book is dedicated to the memory of Bessie Wheeler Gay
and her son, Robert Orvis Gay

Introduction

When I was about thirteen, I discovered a portrait of my grandmother, Bessie. It was under a vanity table in an upstairs bedroom of an aunt's home. From that moment, I felt a strong oneness with this woman who had died nearly ten years before I was born.

As years passed, I developed an interest in genealogy. I began gathering information about my father, Robert's, side of the family. Much later, I started focusing on Bessie. I visited places she lived, searched out town hall records, and researched history of the early 1900s. I persisted in asking questions of my father in the latter years of his life. Without his vivid memories and written pages, I would never have learned about my grandmother's life. For all his stories, maps, diagrams, pictures and inspiration, I owe my deepest gratitude.

I owe my heartfelt thanks, also, to my aunts, Alna Swanson, Mildred Gay, and Orella Colburn and my cousins, Richard and Robert Swanson, who helped immeasurably in the research.

This is an attempt to piece together a biography of one who died before her time but left a strong legacy. She was the predecessor of seven grandchildren, eighteen great-grandchildren and over twenty great-great grandchildren. Although Bessie lived within a range of just a few miles, her descendants have traveled the country and beyond. They span a period of more than a hundred years and have entered the second millennium.

In some instances, especially the Quechee boarding house characters, I have added my own imaginary interpretations because, sadly, no one in the family remains to fill in the missing information.

But with a wealth of facts at hand, I have tried to tell Bessie's story with careful commitment.

Donna D'Addario

Bessie Wheeler Gay

1891 - 1929

The Early Years

Lora, Perly, Alden, Bessie, Lottie, Will
Wheeler

1905

Bessie placed the last of the starched linen napkins on the table, being careful to fold them precisely and set them at the left of the dinner plates just as Mrs. Billings had instructed.

As she turned to go back into the kitchen, she stole a glance out the window. This was the best view of the impressive old woolen mill seated stately on the banks of Dewey's Pond in Quechee. It wouldn't be long before the mill bell would sound and workers would come spilling out of the doors headed toward destinations within traveling distance of this prosperous central Vermont town.

Bessie knew that if she kept watching, she would see her father come out of the box factory, glance across the road to the boarding house and saunter up toward it. How Bessie admired him.

Alden Bisbee Wheeler, or A.B. as he was called, was tall, slim, and had a hint of red in his thinning hair. At fifty-two he was slow and easy going. Beneath his stern exterior there was a sly sense of humor and romance that few knew about, and Bessie treasured those qualities in him. She delighted in recalling stories her mother, Clara Belle, had told her. Stories of how Alden had planned their wedding day to occur on July Fourth of the nation's centennial and how Alden used to tease Clara for breaking so many drinking tumblers. Then one day he bought her a dozen "indestructible" tumblers from a peddler in Woodstock. When he presented this gift to his wife, he had dropped the carton and broken every glass. Stories like these always brought a smile to Bessie's face.

Bessie Maude Wheeler was the youngest of Alden's and Clara's five children. Her two older sisters, Lora and

Lottie, had married and moved to Woodstock. Her brothers, Will and Perly, were not married. Will had bought a farm on Breezy Hill in Prosper and was subject to much speculation because he preferred to live a hermit-like life. Perly, although his desire was to join Will on Breezy Hill, remained home to work and be there for his parents.

Bessie was ten years younger than Perly and Lottie and had held her father's singular attention for many years. Perhaps that is why when Alden had arranged this boarding house job for her, she was willing to comply and do her best to please him even though it meant leaving her mother and home. The boarding house became her new home and gradually she settled into the routine.

Short, plump, chatty Mrs. Billings, who ran the house, had told her, "Missy, you mind your p's and q's, do as you are told and you'll do fine."

Bessie was no stranger to hard work and discipline so the admonition did not trouble her at all. At fourteen, she was a sturdy girl whose body appeared older than her years. She wore her long, light brown hair piled high on top of her head in a fashionable bun. A generous lock fell across her forehead accenting her oval face and delicate features. There was an innocence in her soft blue eyes and no one but Bessie herself knew that on the inside she still possessed the feelings and apprehensions of a young girl.

In the kitchen, Bessie took a deep breath and let the smell of the beef stew flow through her. The steam from the huge black iron pot filled the room with warmth on this cold late winter day. Mrs. Billings was just taking pans of golden biscuits out of the oven. Three heaping apple pies that Bessie had helped prepare earlier were cooling over on the window sills.

This was a homey place and Mrs. Billings ran her house with efficiency. Two other women helped her keep things running smoothly. Mrs. Price, whose husband had died leaving her with a ten-year-old son, was housekeeper. She traveled the mile into Quechee village almost daily by horse and buggy for the mail and supplies at Scott Tinkham's store and saw to other needed errands. She was younger than Mrs. Billings but just as bustling and ambitious.

Then there was Polly who worked only in the kitchen. She was blind in one eye and had a scar near her left temple which she tried to mask by pulling her hair over the spot. She was seventeen and quite childlike. Bessie had heard that Polly was kicked by a milking cow when she was very young and when her own parents wouldn't care for her, Mrs. Billings took her in. Then when Mr. Billings was killed in a mill accident, Mrs. Billings had turned their sprawling home into a boarding house and Polly was a comfort and help.

There it was, the bell declaring the end of another day shift at Dewey's Mill. In this year of 1905, the mill employed over one hundred men producing good woolen cloth called shoddy, shipped to many parts of the world. The huge building, in operation since 1836, was spread over three acres of land at the head of a deep gorge. The mill was powered by an 80 horsepower wheel below a waterfall. The industry drew workers from many miles around and provided livelihood for any able-bodied man. Alden Wheeler had come to work here as a box maker, assembling packing crates for shipping the woolen products.

Bessie heard the voices of the boarders as they shuffled into the large dining room.

"Bessie!" Mrs. Billings' voice arrested her. "Hurry this stew into the big room. The hands are hungry!"

Bessie picked up the heavy tray and took it into the noisy room where twelve men were crowded around the massive mahogany table. She served bowls of stew, biscuits, pitchers of milk and coffee. It seemed as though the men had tireless appetites. As she brought out the slices of pie and chunks of sharp, yellow cheese, some of the men teased her good naturedly about wanting a bigger piece of pie, but the biggest piece she gave quietly to her father.

As the men joked and talked about the events of the day, Bessie noticed one older man glancing her way often. She saw him turn to the man next to him and say something she could not hear but she was sure she heard the other man reply, "That's A.B. Wheeler's young 'un."

Bessie had seen this man before at meals. She had heard the others call him Stillman. She couldn't help but wonder why his eyes were upon her so frequently. Maybe, she mused, I remind him of a daughter or someone. She determined to ask her father about him during a private moment. He would know.

Or George, Mrs. Price's son, would know. Besides attending fifth grade, he was responsible for all the chores at the house. He mowed in the summer, shoveled in the winter, chopped wood and kept the wood box filled. He took care of the horse, made small repairs inside and out, and all the while kept his eyes and ears open to all that was going on around him. Yes, she might ask George about Stillman.

At last, Bessie was free to retire to the tiny back bedroom near the pantry. She shivered as she crawled into the chilly bed. She was exhausted but felt she had accomplished a good day's work. She knew the two dollars she earned for the week would help her family.

*   *   *

5

It snowed six inches during the night. Some of the snow had drifted in and settled on the window sill. Bessie was reluctant to leave the warm covers and start her day, but she washed and dressed swiftly, donning her coat and boots for the dreaded trip out to the privy. The cold bit at her face as she stepped out the back door. She wasted no time going and coming back.

She spotted George plunging his shovel into the thick snow.

"Morning, George."

"Mornin', Miss Bessie. Mighty cold out, ain't it?"

"Why aren't you on your way to school?"

"Teacher's sick. No school today. Ma says I can go skatin' down on the pond soon's I finish shovelin'. Wanna come?"

Bessie smiled. "Sure would love to, but don't have the time. Uh, been meaning to ask you, George. You know that fella Stillman somebody who takes his meals here? Heard he was a clerk at the store. Know who I mean?"

George rested his chin on the shovel handle. "Shore. That'd be Stillman Gay. Started work around these parts couple years ago. Why you ask?"

"Just curious."

"Been married, ya know. Twice! Ain't now though. They both died. First one was from that Lord family in South Woodstock. Carrie, I think. Folks say she died sudden-like with flu. Other one was a Baker. Alna Baker. She took ill and died last February. The man hit on hard luck, I reckon. Ain't got no kids, neither, and he's forty if

6

he's a day. Heard he was born during the war. His Pa went off to fight the South and died down there. He grow'd up never seein' his Pa. Nice enough fella, Gay is. Plays a tuba in the Mill Band. Good hand at dancin', too, old as he is. You settin' your cap for him?"

"No! Certainly not! I was just wondering about him, is all. Don't you tell a soul I was asking, George Price!"

"Not me, Miss Bessie. My lips are sealed. Should he ask, though, can I tell him you're sweet on him?"

Bessie picked up a handful of snow and tossed it at the unsuspecting boy. "Get on with you, George!"

George chuckled, clutched his chest and fell backwards in the snow. Bessie tossed more snow at him as she hurried up the steps into the warm kitchen. She marveled at the wealth of information George had shared.

*   *   *

Several days later, Bessie was carrying a tray of roasted chicken into the dining room just as the boarders were filing in for their evening meal. The man named Stillman was humming to the tune of *In the Good Old Summer Time* as he walked in the door. When he saw Bessie, he stepped in front of her and crooned, "...and will you be my Tootsy-Wootsy in the good old summer time!"

Stillman Orvis Gay
1864 - 1933

Bessie tried to disguise her surprise and embarrassment by stammering, "Get out of my way, you old fool!"

Stillman bowed courteously, laughed, and took his seat at the table. Bessie glanced around the room and spotted her father who seemed to have just a hint of a smile. She set the tray down quickly and retreated to the kitchen where she tried to cool her hot cheeks. Even in her self-consciousness, a smile which she couldn't control tugged at the corners of her mouth. She had to admit he was a rather handsome figure with his trimmed mustache, brown wavy hair and blue-grey eyes that seemed to look right through her.

She tried to avoid looking at him for the rest of the meal but she felt his eyes on her. On his way into the parlor, he came up behind her suddenly while she was clearing the dishes.

"There's a dance in Taftsville Saturday night. Will you be there?"

Bessie didn't know how to answer. She didn't want to appear forward, but she felt compelled to be truthful. "My folks have been planning to go. Perhaps I will be there with them"

"Good. Save me a dance." And Stillman retreated to the parlor with his newspaper. Bessie wondered if he had talked with her father.

Saturday night came. Alden picked up Bessie in a rented buggy with Clara and Perl and they were soon at Thompson's barn. The evening air was brisk but no one minded. Warm blankets covered them from their chins down and once inside the barn, the activity of the dance warmed them.

The caller was in the middle of a rousing square dance. The band consisted of two fiddle players and a banjo player. The music sounded good to Bessie. She loved to dance.

She looked around the room filled with whirling couples and found Stillman dancing with a short, red-haired partner. When the music changed to a waltz, Alden and Clara glided onto the floor. Bessie and Perl watched them with pride. They made such a fine looking couple. Perl gave Bessie a knowing wink.

Suddenly, there was Stillman, whisking Bessie off to the middle of the floor. He was a good dancer. She fairly

9

floated in his strong guiding arms. Throughout the night they danced to Turkey in the Straw, Sailor's Hornpipe, Virginia Reel, and more waltzes. When the caller proclaimed Ladies' Choice, Bessie watched three women hurry up to Stillman. The tall girl in the yellow dress secured the dance with him. How frail she looked, thought Bessie. She shook her head slightly and turned to her father, ceremoniously asking him for a dance. He obliged with a wink as Clara smiled at the two of them. Clara guided her awkward younger son onto the floor.

After that night, there were more Saturday night dances. Sometimes Stillman played his tuba or sang with the bands. He always managed to seek out Bessie and claim several dances. He was becoming bolder at the boarding house, making it public he was interested in her.

One night in mid-March in the middle of a waltz at the Grange Hall, Stillman stopped and guided Bessie over to the coat room where it wasn't so crowded and noisy. He slid his arm around her waist and cleared his throat.

"I spoke my intentions to your father, Bess. He said he wouldn't be contrary to it if you was in agreement. Lord knows I'm some older, but I told him I'd provide for you. A man needs a wife."

Bessie stared up at him with a most incredulous look on her face. He's asking me to marry him, she thought, as the blood raced to her cheeks. She lowered her eyes and tried desperately to think what to say next.

"Well, what's your answer, girl?" Stillman pressed.

"I don't ..., haven't ever... I mean I think I could make you a good wife...." Bessie wasn't sure of what she was saying and the words seemed to be tumbling out of someone else's mouth. She felt angry at herself for sounding so

10

immature and indecisive but Stillman had his answer. He kissed her soundly on her forehead and waltzed her back to the dance floor with a smile.

*   *   *

Bessie never could have imagined in all her girlhood fantasy that, dressed in her navy blue dress and high black shoes, she would be standing beside a man old enough to be her father in the parsonage of the Congregational Church on Elm Street in Woodstock center that cool Saturday afternoon on April Seventeenth in the year 1905.

Alden and Clara and Stillman's lifelong friend, George Buck, stood behind the couple as the Reverend Putnam read the solemn words from a brown book. Bessie felt as though she were living through a dream. She heard the words, "And do you, Stillman Orvis Gay, take Bessie Maude Wheeler to be your lawfully wedded wife?"

All too soon the short ceremony was ended and Bessie's father was hugging her. Her mother was dabbing at her eyes with a lace handkerchief and George Buck was vigorously shaking Stillman's hand. A few more moments of conversation, some money thrust into the hand of the parson, some back slapping, a mother's embrace, and the newlyweds were off and alone for the first time. No grand celebration for Mr. and Mrs. S. O. Gay.

After the wedding, Stillman drove the buggy back to Quechee village to the Lussier home. And there, in their small upstairs room which had been rented by Stillman, they spent their first night together.

Stillman was strong and urgent. Bessie felt awkward and frightened. She was ill-informed about men and such matters. She recalled the only words her mother had ever spoken to her about marriage: "It's hard, Bess, but men must have their way. Try not to make a fuss about it."

And that was all.

Well, she hadn't made a fuss about what occurred that night but as her new husband lay snoring loudly beside her, a silent tear crept slowly down her cheek.

Bessie was happy that Stillman had decided to room at the Lussier's house. Philip and Nelly were an older couple whose neat, white clapboard home was near the center of the village. Bessie felt comfortable with Nelly who was friendly and motherly toward her.

Philip ran the barber shop near Tinkham's general store where Stillman had recently worked delivering groceries with a horse and buckboard. At one time, Philip had given Stillman lessons in barbering, a useful skill to have.

Bessie continued to work daily at the boarding house. Her days were so full since now she was part of the busy activity of the town. She met people – so many people. Farmers and peddlers coming into the village with their wares, townspeople gathered at the bandstand for summer concerts, church goers at the meeting house services, mill workers, neighbors. Every day was a new adventure for her.

*   *   *

On a frosty January morning, Bessie shivered as she put her feet down on the bare wooden floor. She felt a sensation in her stomach that she didn't like. She tried to dismiss this sickish feeling as she hurried into her clothes. Stillman was already on his way to the mill where he had taken a job as a repairman because the pay was better.

Bessie quickly made the bed, washed her face, and went down stairs to tell Nelly that she didn't want breakfast this morning. Maybe just a sip of black coffee.

She buckled on her galoshes and stepped out into the cold air. The sick feeling returned and the mile trudge to the boarding house seemed much longer than usual. Perhaps that rhubarb cobbler last night didn't agree with me, she reasoned.

Mrs. Billings was stoking the wood in the stove and Polly was seated at the table peeling carrots when Bessie walked in kicking the snow off her boots and unwrapping her wool scarf. They turned to greet her.

"Feels raw out there this morning," declared Bessie.

"Ayuh. Stiff wind whistlin' up through the gorge. Expectin' more snow by nightfall. You look a mite peaked. You feelin' poorly?" Mrs. Billings asked.

"Well," Bessie confessed, "I do feel a little under the weather today. Must be something I ate. Hope it's not the grippe."

"Ooo, Miz Bessie Gay," Polly cooed, "must be in the family way! I heard my ol' Ma speak of it once. She said she was like to spill out her stomach with the sickness. Best stay close to the privy!"

"Land sakes, Polly! You let Bessie be. Don't pay her any mind, child. What's to be will be. Come near the stove and warm yourself."

In the family way. Bessie mulled over those words. She had only known womanhood for a little over a year. In the family way? Could it be?

*   *   *

When she was four and a half months into her pregnancy and just beginning to show, Bessie decided it was time to tell Stillman. To her surprise, he was elated and told everyone about the strapping son he expected to have as though he himself were carrying the child. He even

14

fashioned a wooden cradle during the months of waiting and carved the initials J.O.G. on the headboard to stand for James Orvis, his son.

On October Fifth, Bessie went into hard labor early in the morning. Nelly sent Philip for the town doctor and stayed close by Bessie's bed, wiping her brow and giving her words of encouragement. Stillman paced back and forth in the little room until Nelly ordered him to pace downstairs.

Three hours later, the strong cries of a baby were heard upstairs and down. Stillman came running. Bessie managed to lift her head to see Nelly swaddling the baby in a cotton blanket.

"It's a girl, Bess! It's a girl! And a big one she is!"

Bessie was shaking uncontrollably, her hair was matted and damp, and tears made her eyes blurry but she attempted a smile before falling back on the pillow in complete exhaustion.

She sensed that Stillman was concealing his disappointment. "Well," he quipped, "she'll be my Jim!"

He named their daughter Alna. He didn't say why, but Bessie knew. Alna was the name of his second wife whose memory he still harbored. Bessie favored the name Julia after her father's mother, but she didn't tell Stillman.

Alden and Clara were so moved and excited by their youngest daughter's achievement, that they made a quick visit with gifts to welcome their new nearly twelve-pound granddaughter.

Bessie regained her strength quickly and baby Alna flourished.

The year was saddened only by the death of Bessie's maternal grandmother, Margaret Stevens.

Bessie often thought about how her grandparents' home in East Barnard always had been filled with music. Margaret had played the organ. Her daughter, Lizzie, was known to have one of the best contralto voices in the area. Her son, Collins, who had moved to Marietta, Ohio to manufacture church and parlor organs was also a good singer. And Clara, who learned to play piano from her mother, taught Bessie to play at a very early age.

It was said that one of their ancestors, Andrew Stevens, who was a Methodist minister, had a remarkable voice as well. Music was an important part of life for the Stevens family.

The passing of Margaret, the last of Bessie's grandparents, was a great loss to Bessie.

1908

In September of 1908, Alna was a chubby toddler and Bessie was heavy with child again.

Stillman had a worried look as he came in the door from work one night.

"Mother's taken sick. Doctors can't say what it is. Just has no strength at all. And Bill's rheumatiz is getting' worse all the time. He can't manage the farm by himself anymore. Looks like we'll have to move up there. I've given my notice at the mill and can leave at the end of the week. What do you say?

Bessie knew no answer was necessary. Stillman had already made up his mind and put his plan into action.

It was a sad day when Bessie had to say goodbye to Nelly and the friends she'd made in Quechee. Stillman hired a horse and buckboard at the livery stable and packed their few belongings. Nelly gave Alna a little squeeze on her cheek.

"Shore gonna miss this sweet child. Ain't so far away you can't keep in touch, don't you know."

Bessie waved to Nelly as Stillman turned the horse down the hill, through the covered bridge and away from Quechee. They traveled along the Ottaquechee River road through Taftsville and Woodstock then headed west to Bridgewater. There, they crossed the river at the woolen mill and turned up Curtis Hollow Road. About five miles up on a road that became narrower and less traveled, they stopped at their destination.

The Dugan place was where Stillman had been born, so for him it was coming home. But this lonesome place far up in the valley in Reading seemed twenty miles from nowhere to Bessie.

As they turned into the driveway, Stillman's step-father, Bill Dugan, stopped pitching hay into the barn long enough to wave. His wife, Roana, was sitting in a rocker on the front porch, snapping beans into a colander in her lap. Bessie studied her mother-in-law for a moment and thought how frail she looked since the last time she'd seen her. At sixty-eight, her hair was grey, she was thin, and seemed even shorter than her five-foot stature.

"Wall, if it ain't the Gays come to call." Roana didn't rise from her chair but she put down the colander and reached out her arms.

"Let me hold my gran'baby."

Bessie placed squirming Alna in Roana's lap.

"Hello, Mother Dugan. She's a heavy one lately. Always on the go, too."

Stillman emptied the buggy of the valises and boxes and then stabled the horse. They moved into the side rooms that had windows looking north toward Richmond Hill. Bessie liked the view.

As September rolled into October, Bessie and Stillman fell into the routine of farm life. Stillman and Bill did the milking, finished the harvesting and haying, set in meat for winter, made repairs, banked the house, and even found a little time for bird hunting.

Bessie worked from dawn to dusk filling canning jars, making pickles and preserves, cooking meats, feeding the

18

hens and looking after Alna. Roana helped with what strength she had and never complained about the tiredness that was plaguing her.

Bessie made time every few days to spend some moments in Roana's flower garden pulling out weeds and admiring the display of fall colors of the mums and zinnias. She savored the last bursts of color, knowing snow would soon cover the valley with a colorless blanket.

*   *   *

She saw that she wasn't gaining as much weight as when she was carrying Alna but she felt strong and her appetite was keen. Besides, the new baby wasn't due until December so she had time yet. Stillman scarcely mentioned her state. His chores kept him away from the house most of the day and he fell into bed each night obviously weary to the bone.

*   *   *

On a grey afternoon early in November, Bessie was taking the wash off the line. As she bent over to put the overalls in the basket, she felt a sharp pain. Hurriedly, she took down the last of the clothes, picked up the overflowing basket and carried it into the kitchen. Another pain came as she set the basket down. This time she cried out.

Roana left the soup she was stirring and came to Bessie's side just as she fell back into a chair clutching her stomach.

"What is it, Bess?" Roana's face showed alarm. "Is it time?"

Bessie straightened up as the pain subsided. "I'm not due for another month."

19

"You've been pushing yourself too hard taking on all the work. And me not pulling my load. Let me fix you a cup of sassafras tea. Might help whatever ails you." Roana lit the fire under the kettle.

Alna began to fuss in the parlor where she was just waking up from her nap. Bessie started to go attend to her when another pain seized her.

"We best get Stillman in here. You get to bed," Roana ordered.

Stillman came rushing in from the barn. "What's wrong?"

"Something's amiss," Roana answered. "She's too early. I don't 'spect we have time to get that Dr. Cram way up here. Go fetch Hatty Ocean. She'll know what to do. Hurry, Stillman!"

At seven o'clock that night, Bessie heard the feeble cries of her first-born son. Tiny, red, wrinkled and only three and a half pounds, Bessie and Stillman stared upon this frail soul and exchanged a look of hopelessness.

Their neighbor Hatty Ocean was the only one with any optimism. "Now mind me, you wrap that boy good. Bring me a shoe box or the like. We'll set him on the end of the stove by the reservoir and he'll be as warm as toast. He'll prosper. You mark my words."

Day after day, the tiny baby in a shoe box was kept on the warm stove in the kitchen. Dr. Cram of Bridgewater came by a few days later and checked him over.

"Yep. This boy will make it if he don't get croup or somethin'. You nursin' okay? Keep him warm. He'll come along."

Three weeks went by and the baby gained steadily. By the end of the fifth week, he weighed almost seven pounds and was demanding more and more feeding time.

"I reckon if we're gonna get to keep him, we may as well give the little feller a name," said Stillman.

So Frank Arthur was named at last.

*   *   *

It was a long, cold, quiet winter. Bessie found joy in caring for inquisitive Alna and her infant son but she missed Quechee and Nelly. Most of all she missed her parents. The roads were practically impassable during those frozen months.

She passed her eighteenth birthday in January. Nobody noticed but Bessie. She remembered when her sister, Lottie, turned the same age. She had become engaged to Mr. Churchill.

"And here I have a husband and two babies already," she mused.

Evenings were filled sitting by lamp light mending, sewing for the children, and quilting. Roana helped some but her hands were becoming increasingly crippled and it was painful for her to hold a needle. Bessie's greatest enjoyment was to listen to Roana reminisce about Stillman's real father whose name was also Stillman Orvis but he was better known as Orvis.

"Those were the days of the war between the North and South," Roana would recount. "Never thought it would touch us up here in the hills of Vermont. But when President Lincoln called for help to keep the nation together, Vermont got involved by pledging a million dollars and giving up 35,000 of our men and boys to the cause. Orvis and I were married and had young ones. Hamden was eight. The girls, younger. Nothing doing but Orvis had to go to war, too. He left me with all the children and me expecting Stillman here. He went off on Christmas Day in '63 and that was the last I saw of him. Stillman, you was born nine days later on January second. Those was hard times. I didn't care about some ol' war. I just wanted my man back.

"I got one letter mid-January saying the fighting was going good. He told how he was in a company of sharpshooters. Always was a good shot, as I remember. He'd got my letter telling about Stillman and said he'd be home soon to see his new son.

"One night, at the end of March, plain as day I had this dream, or vision, or whatever you want to call it. Anyway, I heard sand being shoveled against the house. Ayuh, sand right in winter. Well, a few days later comes this telegram saying my man is dead. Buried someplace down Virginia. He'd got bad sick and taken to a hospital camp. They brought in a soldier with small pox and the camp was 'bout wiped out from it. My Orvis was one who got it, weak as he was. The gov'ment wrote that he was a good soldier. I recollect that about five thousand volunteers lost their lives to the cause and those were just Vermonters. So I wasn't alone. But we were in a bad fix till ol' Bill here come along. He took us all on as family and then added more to our brood, right Bill?"

Bill and Stillman listened to Roana's tales with interest. They spent their evenings repairing and sharpening tools. Bill generally fell asleep the second his head tilted

22

back in the rocker if Stillman didn't keep him awake by prodding him into a game of checkers.

Stillman whittled toys for the children and made a little sled to pull Alna around in the snow. One night he carved a wooden train engine with wheels and attached a pull string.

"Look, Jim," he explained as he handed it to his daughter. "This is like the train your old Dad used to work on."

Alna giggled with delight while it clattered behind her across the floor.

*　　*　　*

Spring finally came to the valley. After the long thaw and the mud season, buds appeared on branch and stem.

Bessie began looking for reasons to be outside more. She took Alna for little discovery walks where she pointed out tiny purple, white and yellow violets. At the edge of the woods on the fern-clad damp ground she showed her yellow hepatica, jack-in-the-pulpits, adder's tongue, and brilliant red trillium also known as stinking Benjamin. She cautioned Alna not to pick God's lovely creations but to enjoy the beauty and fragrances.

As the days grew warmer and Bessie could escape from her other duties, she made time to nurture Roana's flower garden. As the children played nearby, she would sing hymns as she worked. Sometimes the children would hum along with her.

Summer meant occasional Sunday rides to Woodstock and even once in a while, to Quechee to visit 'Aunt Nelly.'

How Bessie loved the long rides to see family and show off the children.

The children were thriving like the weeds in her garden. Time passed swiftly. And the days ebbed into years at the Dugan place in Reading.

In 1912 Roana Dugan died in her sleep. Stillman controlled any emotion he felt but Bessie and six-year old Alna wept unashamedly.

Roana was buried in a cemetery on the road to North Bridgewater in the same plot with her daughter, Birdie, who had died at the tender age of eleven.

Once again Bessie had to say goodbye. This time to a dear friend and companion.

That winter was long and lonely without Roana for company. Bill, seventy-one and grieving his loss, was able to do less and less on the farm. Bessie and Stillman managed to keep everything running through the spring and summer.

One hot day Stillman came back from town, unhitched the wagon and coaxed the stubborn ox into the stall. He brought in the supplies and thrust the newspaper in front of Bessie.

"Look at this, will ya! Henry Ford is puttin' out those Model T's of his, a thousand a day. A day, mind you! And says there's been a big flood out in Ohio. Ain't that where your Uncle Collins has that factory? Hope he didn't get bad hit. Flood's a terrible thing."

*   *   *

In September, Alna, now almost seven, entered first grade at Curtis Hollow School. It was hard for Bessie to let her go. And the three-mile walk to the one-room schoolhouse was no short journey for a small, shy girl.

A few days after school started, Alna came home visibly shaking with tears in her eyes. Bessie sat her down, wiped her eyes and asked what had happened.

"I was walking past the ledges," Alna sniffed, "and a whole herd of deer ran right in front of me. They scared me bad. Almost coulda kilt me! Made so much noise! Please don't make me go back there again!"

After that, Bessie determined to walk more than half way with her in the morning and to meet her coming home as well.

On a beautiful October afternoon, Bessie got a late start walking down Mecawee Road to meet Alna. She took Frank with her and they walked the half mile to the huge yellow birch tree. Then they spotted Alna trudging along. Quickly, she and Frank slipped behind the tree and hid until Alna was close by.

Bessie and Frank jumped from behind the tree. Bessie said, "Boo!" And she and Frank started laughing.

Alna was startled and began to cry. Sobbing, she declared angrily, "You scart me! Don't do that ever again!"

Bessie felt repentant and gave her a hug, but the sniffling continued all the way home.

Frank couldn't contain his snickering. Apparently it was the funniest thing ever a mother could do. And hearing his big sister sob made it all the funnier.

Bessie decided never to try that again.

Near the end of the year, Bessie received a letter from her mother. How she relished news from home. In this message, Clara had exciting news to share with her daughter.

It seemed that Clara's brother, Collins, had given one of the organs from his factory to the church in East Barnard in memory of Bessie's grandmother, Margaret Manning Stevens, who died on Christmas day in 1906. Clara wrote that the organ had the words 'Stevens – Marietta, Ohio" stamped right on it.

Bessie let the news sink in. What a good thing for a son to do to perpetuate the memory of his mother, she thought. She was eager to go see the organ in the church where she had worshipped years ago.

East Barnard Church which houses Stevens organ

Clara went on in her letter to tell about the flood that ravaged Ohio where Collins was living. She said that when the Ohio River overflowed and caught people by surprise, Collins took refuge in the cupola of the factory. For three days he was constrained to stay in the safety of the small structure. But he emerged without a scratch.

Bessie hastily wrote a note back thanking her mother for the news and telling her stories about Alna and Frank and life in Reading.

By late winter, Bill had decided he couldn't face another year of planting and maintaining the farm. With Stillman's help, he made some contacts and sold the farm for lumbering rights. He auctioned off his livestock and household goods and moved to White River Junction to live with his younger son, Gilbert, or Idey as he was called.

Stillman had been making inquiries in Bridgewater and had learned that the boarding house across from the woolen mill was in need of new management. That he had never run a boarding house before did not concern him. It was a good paying job and he was up to the challenge.

"You've done this work before," he reasoned when he broke the news to Bessie about his decision. "The kids won't be so far from school and there will be people around again. You'll like that, won't you?"

He moved Bessie, the children and all their belongings into that boarding house. Within a week they had begun their new task of managing the place. Bessie didn't like being uprooted again but she did like being in the center of town where once again there was activity.

The new job promised to be a good business venture because of the woolen mill which had been in existence since the 1820's. It had manufactured blankets during the Civil War and continued to employ around one hundred and fifty people. That kept the boarding house constantly busy.

For Bessie, the duties were familiar and natural. This was a bigger house than the one at Dewey's Mill, but the tasks were the same. Feed twenty-five men each evening and keep ten rooms neat and clean. With Stillman's help as cook, baker and handyman, the routine started falling into place.

One month after they began their new position, Bessie suffered an early miscarriage. She resolved that nothing could be profited by telling Stillman so she kept the loss to herself.

"Lord," she prayed, "You know this is not a time to be having new babies, what with all the work just starting. I thank You for knowing best." But she ached for the child that was never to be.

The children were adjusting to their new environment well. As time went on, Bessie was able to hire Mrs. Frasier from Bridgewater Corners to give Alna lessons on the parlor piano. Alna objected to the practicing, but Bessie insisted.

"I learned to play as a girl your age and so shall you."

Frank would stand by the piano during Alna's lessons and after Mrs. Frasier would leave, he would finger the notes he remembered hearing. He was able to pick out simple tunes by ear.

Since Sundays were quieter days with roomers off visiting relatives for the day, Bessie was able to slip away with the children to the Congregational church just a few doors down the street. There she received the right hand of fellowship and the children learned their Bible stories. Alna couldn't wait for Sundays to come but Frank didn't like dressing up. He pleaded to stay home with his father. Bessie, however, slicked his hair back and took him by the hand every Lord's Day.

Bridgewater Congregational Church

One Sunday they returned to find Stillman outside splitting wood.

"Well, what did the good reverend go on about today? Did he whip us back-slidden sinners as usual?"

Bessie managed a smile. "Wouldn't hurt you to come along, Father. The Lord wants even the likes of you," she teased.

"Well, now. When the Lord wants to come help with the chores around here, I'll make Him a deal."

Bessie shot him a look of disdain. "Hush that talk now!" And she swiftly guided the children into the house to change their Sunday clothes.

*   *   *

On a clear summer afternoon, Alna and Frank were playing hide and seek outside. They giggled and ran in and out of the house looking for new and challenging places to hide.

After a while, Alna ran into the dining room where Bessie was setting the table for supper.

"Did you see Frank go through here? She asked. "He's hiding and I can't find him anywhere. I don't want to play anymore."

31

"Don't you worry. He'll show up for suppertime. Frank never misses vittles," and Bessie continued her chore.

But Frank didn't appear by supper. By now Bessie and Stillman were becoming frantic. They even enlisted the boarders to help in the search. Bessie's biggest fear was the Ottaquechee River across the road. People scoured all the buildings nearby as well as the river.

Bessie searched inside the whole house. As she made one more pass through the kitchen, she heard a cry coming from under the sink. She opened the cupboard door and there he was, all curled up and yawning from sleep. Relief flooded over her and her knees suddenly felt weak. She called Stillman. He stopped short at the sight of his son huddled under the sink and snatched him up.

"Whatever possessed you to crawl in there? We've been half crazy looking for you! I ought to whip your hide for a stunt like that!"

Stillman was angry and Alna was shaking. Bessie wrung her hands not knowing what to do.

Frank cocked his head and looked into his father's eyes. "Alna didn't find me, did she?"

Bessie called the boarders back in for supper.

Besides talk of Frank's escapade that early August evening, the bigger subject for conversation was news of Great Britain's declaration of war against Germany on the fourth.

The Curtis Hollow Years

Painting by Robert O. Gay

Frank and Alna were growing fast. Life at the boarding house was busy, but good. Bessie continued to enjoy attending church just a few steps away. And she liked being surrounded by the bustle of activity in town. Because the Mill employed people from a wide radius, she heard news from outside of Bridgewater. Stories the mill workers told were always of interest to her. It was on a cool day in September that Stillman brought some news that would again alter Bessie's life.

Supper was over. The boarders had settled in for the evening. Bessie and Stillman were still in the kitchen putting boysenberry pies together for the next day. Frank and Alna were in bed in their upstairs room.

Stillman spoke. "Happened to be talkin' to Alby Curtis today. He says the Gustav Curtis place is up for sale. Sounds like t'might be a good deal. Three hundred and sixty acres just above the turn to Lake Macawee. Close to school and good farm land." He paused before going on.

"Thought I'd take a run up there and have a look."

Bessie sighed inwardly. She was tired. At twenty-five, she was becoming less resilient. A farm with over three hundred acres? The thought was overwhelming at this time of day, but she tried to sound interested.

"What do you s'pose they want for it?"

"Dunno. Didn't ask. Thought I'd look first. Always wanted to own a place. Frank's getting bigger now. He'd be a good deal a'help with chores, and we can't stay here forever. It's already taking its toll on your health."

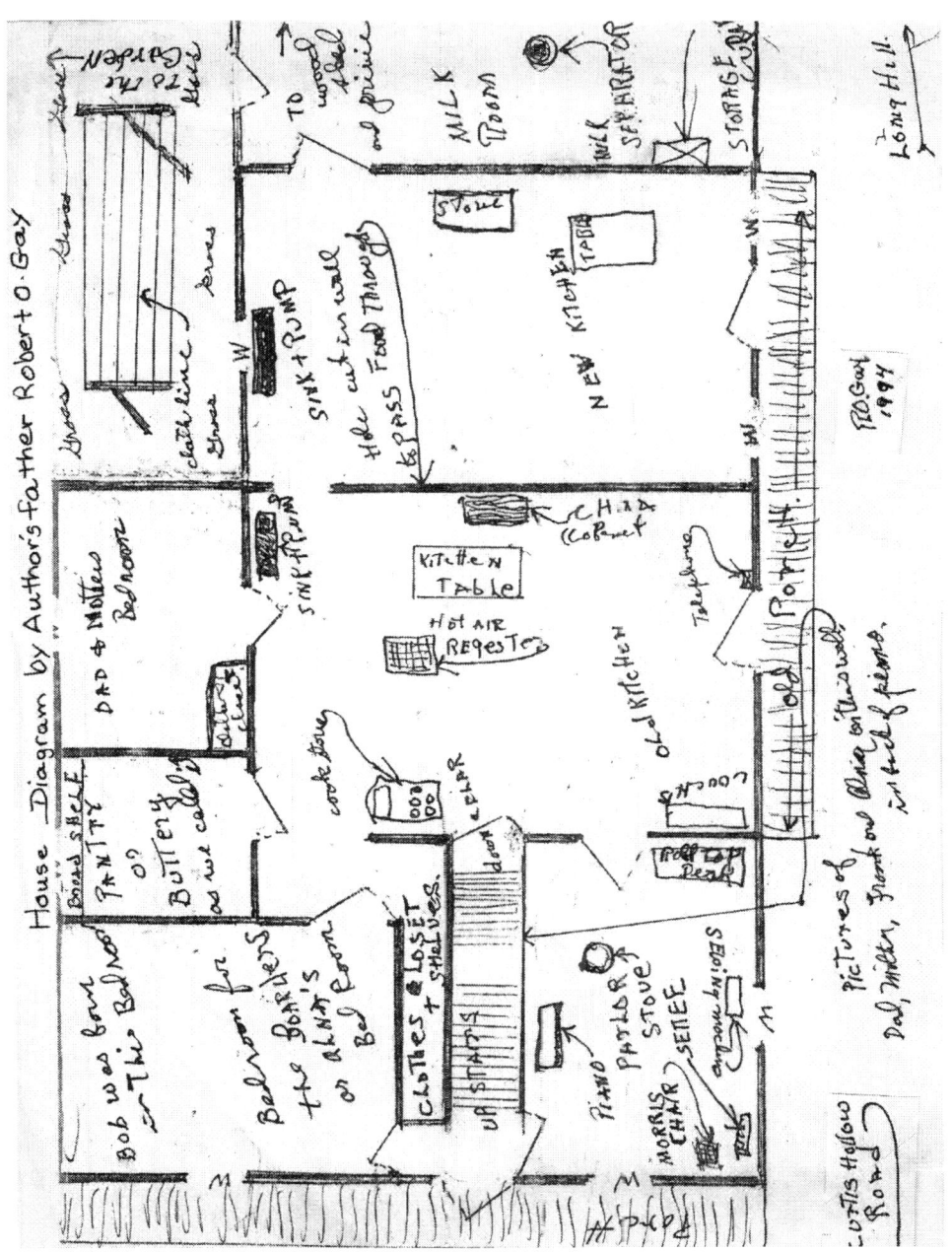

House Diagram by Author's Father Robert O. Gay

That was the end of the conversation, but a few days later, Stillman reported back to Bessie that Frank Tayler had given him a ride up the valley to look over the Curtis place.

"I think it'll do us. The price is right. Wants five hundred for it, stock and all. Sounds like it's time to make the move."

Within a few weeks, Bessie and Stillman made the transition from boarding house managers to farm owners.

*   *   *

The farm was two and a half miles up the Curtis Hollow valley road, nestled at the foot of Long Hill to the east and Bald Mountain to the south. The Curtis Hollow Brook snaked through the property on its way down to where it emptied into the Ottaquechee.

The acreage was made up of hay fields, pasture land, orchards, hard wood, and fertile fields for tilling. The house and out buildings were set close to the road just a half mile uphill from the school. Some old pieces of farm equipment, ten Guernsey cows, a pair of oxen, a tired plow horse, three fat hogs, and some laying hens were included in the transaction. The vacant and noticeably run-down Clement place up the road on the right was also part of the package.

Bert Curtis's farm spread out just below the school and hugged Stillman's northern boundary. Ben Smith's place bordered the south side. The bulk of the land in the Hollow was owned by Curtis families. Miles of stone fences wound through the valley separating the farms.

After ten years of living in other people's houses, Bessie was elated to have a home of her own. The two-story white house had a porch across the front that opened into a roomy kitchen. The ample-sized pantry and two bedrooms comprised the back of the house. One bedroom was for Alna and the larger for Bessie and Stillman.

The parlor faced the southwest side, and Bessie could watch the sun set over Richmond Hill from the window facing the road. In the parlor were a settee, a Morris chair, her sewing machine, a round heat stove, and her beloved piano which had belonged to her mother. Upstairs were two bedrooms, one of which was Frank's, and a spacious storage area.

The kitchen led to the milk room. An enclosed walkway behind the attached wood and wagon sheds led to the privy on the east end of the house.

Beyond the wagon shed were the hen houses, hay barn and stable. A stone wall bordered the barnyard, enclosing the pigpen and water trough.

The self-supporting farm demanded labor from early dawn to last light. Stillman, at fifty, was strong and capable. Frank, now seven, was able to work beside his father watching, learning and obeying Stillman's stern commands.

Bessie and Alna kept the house, stock and garden and helped with haying. Although the work was hard and constant, it was continually changing. And each season brought its own rewards.

This was home now to Bessie and her family.

Bessie heard Alna and Frank noisily coming through the milk room and appeared in the kitchen with excited looks on their faces.

Alna spoke first. "We brought the cows home, Mother. But we got scart up on the hill."

"Yeah," chimed in Frank, "there was a bobcat or somepin' up in the hemlock trees. It screamed and made a turrable sound. We druv those ol' cows home in a hurry, we did!"

"It was an awful scary noise. Wish those cows wouldn't wander so far up that hill," Alna added.

"Father says they go to the top of Long Hill because it's cooler," Bessie reminded them. She stopped to look at her children. Frank, growing taller and reedier by the day, and his hair beginning to show traces of red. He put her in mind of her own father.

And Alna. Nearing ten and short for her age with a roundness to her body. Her curly brown hair clung to her face on this warm afternoon.

"My, if you don't resemble your Grandma Dugan on the Gay side of the family, Alna."

Alna smiled. It obviously pleased her to hear those words. "You recollect how Grandma used to wear two aprons—one in front and one in back? And she'd switch the clean white one to the front if company'd come? 'Member, Mother?"

Bessie remembered very clearly.

That summer Bessie learned that her mother was suffering from an infection resulting from an earlier incident when she had stepped on a rusty nail. For her treatments, it was necessary to travel to Hanover hospital in New Hampshire. After each treatment, she stayed a few days at the farm with Bessie. Bessie, of course, was delighted to have her mother there and relished every moment of their time together.

She rarely saw any of her family now that she resided in the Hollow. If there was visiting, it was more often to see Stillman's side of the family. His sisters, Alice and Mary, and his half-brothers, Edgar and Idey.

1917

Bessie was bent over the huge black boiling kettle washing clothes. Even though it was early April, the perspiration ran down the sides of her face in little rivulets. It was hard work wringing out the woolen overalls, and the heaviness of her body in the sixth month of pregnancy made the work even more arduous.

Stillman, returning from town, turned the oxen into the yard. He waved a newspaper at her and called, "It's war, Bess! We're in it now for sure! President Wilson just declared it!" He unyoked the team and dragged the buggy into the shed.

Bessie wiped her forehead with the back of her hot, red hand. It seemed strange to her to imagine the United States getting involved in fighting going on over in Europe. Could all that war talk touch her here in Curtis Hollow? Stillman, she rationalized, was too old to go to war. And surely the U.S. would settle the problem with those Germans long before her son was of age. Somebody else would have to do the fighting. Other wives' husbands. Other mothers' sons. She closed her eyes as she considered the pain they would know and whispered a prayer. She felt a twinge of conscience as she recalled stories her parents had told her about Wheeler and Stevens ancestors who fought bravely in the Revolutionary War and even in King Phillip's War of 1675. She thought of Stillman's father who died fighting the Civil War, but she forced these thoughts quickly from her mind as she carried the heavy basket of wet clothes to the line.

Talk of war dominated the conversation of men who came and went from Bessie's house throughout the spring and into the hot summer. However, Bessie's mind was occupied with the growth of the child inside her and the dwindling health of her mother. Since Alden and Clara were living in Quechee, Bessie saw little of them. She knew that her mother, who had just turned sixty-five, was growing increasingly weaker.

*   *   *

Friday, July twenty-seventh, was hot like most late summer days but Bessie minded it more because she was in labor. Alna wrung out rags in cool water in a basin and applied them to her mother's forehead, neck and arms. Bessie's whole body was swollen, and as she writhed on the bed, the heat made her condition intolerable. The pains were steady now. Only minutes apart. She just wanted this baby out.

Moments later she heard the screen door slam and heard Dr. Cram's voice call out, "Miz Gay!"

Alna led the doctor with his small black bag into the back bedroom. Bessie let out a heart-chilling scream.

Two hours later, Bessie was delivered of her child. A healthy boy weighing twelve pounds and eleven ounces. Bessie, exhausted and weak, fell back on the pillow with the clean wrapped baby beside her.

Alna ran excitedly out to the barn to bring in Stillman and Frank. They looked in awe upon the chubby, red-faced newborn.

Dr. Cram packed the last of his instruments into his bag and said, "Well, Mr. Gay, this one's big enough to put to work in the hay field if you could find a pair of britches big enough to fit 'im!"

41

Seventeen days after the birth of Robert Orvis, Bessie received the devastating news that her mother had died. Still in a weakened condition, she was heart-broken and cried uncontrollably. She wished she could have been with Clara the afternoon she slipped away. No amount of logic could dispel her guilt.

The family attended the funeral service two days later. Bessie leaned on Alna for support and stayed close to her father, Alden. Frank stood tall beside Stillman. Bessie's brothers and sisters were there as well as a few friends of the Wheeler family.

Clara was buried atop a hill overlooking Quechee village. Through misty eyes, Bessie looked around and thought how serene the place was. But she felt her mother was so alone, and she could scarcely stand the pain. She cuddled little Robert closer to her breast.

*   *   *

October was the most beautiful month in the valley. The hills were ablaze with brilliant orange, red and yellow set against a background of sky so blue it seemed unreal. Bessie thought, God must paint this spectacular canvas as a gift of hope to remember through the colorless months ahead.

She inhaled the fragrance of apples and burning leaves as she stepped out to the edge of the road on a late Friday afternoon. She placed her hand above her eyes as a visor and squinted to see as far as she could down the road. The sun was beginning to slip down behind the hills. Frank should have been home from school by now.

Until a little while ago she hadn't been concerned, even though Stillman had come looking for him several times.

42

She had reminded him that Frank often stayed behind to help the teacher put out the fire in the stove, clean the blackboard and close up for the weekend.

She stood and watched until the sun was gone and went back into the house. She met Stillman coming into the kitchen from the milk room. He was visibly upset. "Is he home yet?"

Bessie shook her head and pumped some water into the kettle.

"I'm goin' down to that school now and I best not find him dawdlin' along the way or he'll get a lesson he shan't forget!"

He grabbed a lantern and stormed out while Bessie tried to keep her mind on supper. Alna, who was sitting at the table peeling apples, knew nothing of her brother's whereabouts.

A little more than half an hour later, Frank came through the door, red-faced and sullen.

"Where have you been? I've been most out of my mind with worry. And your father is on his way down to fetch you home!"

Alna put down the knife she was using and listened with interest to Frank's reply.

"Teacher kept me afta school 'cause I wouldn't squeal on Donald Snow. He didn't do nawthin', neither. She got mad. Then it got dark and she got madder 'cause now she was scar't to walk home. That's when Dad burst in and hollered and swatted me on the head. He sent me packin' and told Miss Bagly he would hafta walk her home so's no bears would get 'er in the dark!"

Frank was breathless and angry. Bessie laid her hand tenderly on Frank's shoulder. "Go to the barn and carry in the milk cans before your father gets back. Then wash up and eat your vittles."

When Stillman came home, his portion of the meal was on the stove and Bessie served it to him. The long walk in the dark had settled him down.

He just muttered, "Durned woman. Ought to hire a man for the job a 'teachin'."

Frank stayed out of his way and went upstairs to bed early.

Bessie loved spring in the valley. Even the loathsome mud that came after the winter thaw didn't dash her enthusiasm. There was hope in the air. Color was returning. Birds returned after long months of absence. The brook, swollen and free, gurgled joyfully as it tumbled down its path. There were new fragrances. And even the fields, plowed and fertilized, had the pungent aroma of promise that spring brings.

She was glad that the two lumbermen who had boarded with them during the winter months were gone now and she could care for just her family of five again. Robert was not yet three and required close attention. She was grateful for Alna's help when she was not in school.

Stillman was starting to show signs of aging. His joints ached in the morning, and it was harder for him to put in a long day's work. He smiled less often at home and was subject to fits of rage when a member of the family didn't live up to his expectations. He took much of his anger out on Frank who was now nearly the size of Stillman. Bessie shuddered when he took the strap to Frank, but she knew better than to interfere because his rage would increase. She tried to make up for Stillman's severe discipline by spending time with Frank at bedtime. She enjoyed these talks with her big son as much as she felt he needed the comfort and assurance.

Bessie knew that some of Stillman's behavior had to do with his occasional access to liquor. Now that prohibition was a law, men seemed to become more aware of their desire to drink. Stillman was no exception. Four or five times a year he was able to get a supply of corn liquor or hard cider from Ben Smith or friends from town. At those times, Bessie and the children knew they were in for bad times.

But this particular early morning in May was not one of those times. This day Stillman had a task for the family. He laid out the plan as Bessie served up breakfast of fried potatoes, oatmeal, biscuits, gravy and coffee. Frank walked in the back doorway.

"Milkin' done?" Stillman's question was assumed more than asked.

Frank nodded and sat down to eat.

"Eat up. We're goin' to the Clement place today to tear down and haul that lumber back for the new barn. Got a few days to plantin' and I want that barn finished afore winter sets in. Bert says he'll give me a hand with the roof when the time comes."

"Good deal of work," Bessie responded, "but that old place should be easy enough to take apart. It's been falling down for years."

"Jim," Stillman's nickname for Alna, "you slop the hogs for your mother and turn the cows out. Frank, hitch up the team to the hay wagon while I run the milk cans down to Bert's. Mother, fix up some dinner pails and stuff Robert in your apron pocket. Long day ahead."

Later that morning the whole family was engaged in tearing out doors and windows in the house and barn and stripping lumber down. Everything was piled into the long hay wagon – every salvageable scrap. Little Robert helped carry short planks and picked up nails until he tired and fell asleep beneath a purple lilac bush.

It took two long days of filling and unloading the wagon, but the job was finished and there was a corporate sigh of relief with shared blisters and splinters.

Robert and Alna

Bessie tucked Robert into bed in her room and collapsed on the settee. She glanced at the bold headline of the newspaper: VERMONT WOMEN GET VOTE!

Well, she thought, about time. Maybe what this country needs is a woman's voice in government. We work alongside the men. Seems like we should vote with them, too.

The kerosene lamp light flickered throughout the room; she dozed off with her mending basket left untouched in her lap.

*   *   *

The addition to the barn went up slowly that summer in between periods of planting, haying and harvesting. Bert Curtis, from the farm below, came up when he could spare the time and helped Stillman with the beams and the roof.

Bert was thirty-five and a self-proclaimed bachelor. He was bearded with red hair. Bessie admired Bert. He was not given to much small talk, but had an engaging wit and a twinkle in his eyes. She knew him to be a fair man. He was known throughout the valley for his willingness to give a helping hand. He loaned money with just a handshake, and was heard to say, "If a fella doesn't pay me back, it's worth the loss to know the value of a man's word."

Bert did all the butchering in the valley and farmers paid him in beef or pork. He also transported neighbors' milk cans filled with cream each morning to Bridgewater to meet the milk truck. Bessie knew this was a great convenience for Stillman.

In winter, the state paid Bert to plow the Hollow road with his unusual invention of two spruce trees chained to the sides of a bobsled. He kept the road snow-packed and serviceable after severe storms. He was a valuable man in the valley and a friend to everyone.

Bessie often invited him and his white-haired, bewhiskered father, Albert, for Sunday dinners. She enjoyed feeding Bert because he was so appreciative and had a voracious appetite. Before leaving, he always would say, "Much obliged for the vittles. See ya, the good Lord willin'."

It was after one Sunday dinner of rabbit meat pie in late October that the barn addition was officially finished. Stillman handed Frank a pail of tar and a brush and held the ladder while Frank climbed up on the roof. While the family and Bert watched, Frank carefully painted the year 1920 with large brush strokes across the top. Bessie and Alna clapped as Frank descended.

The following afternoon, Frank brought the cows home and he and Stillman led them into their new stables.

* * *

Throughout that October, there had been much discussion about the running mates in the upcoming election. Calvin Coolidge, the Governor of Massachusetts, had lost the Republican nomination to Warren Harding. But he was chosen to run with Harding as vice-president. Coolidge was a favorite among Vermonters because he was born and brought up in the village of Plymouth just a few miles over the hill to the west.

The Democrat candidates were James Cox of Ohio and Franklin Delano Roosevelt of New York. Stillman's comment was, "Whoever heard of this Cox fella and Roosevelt afore this election come up? Where do they find 'em!"

Bessie knew it wouldn't make a difference even if those candidates were well-known. They were Democrats. And everyone knew Vermonters were staunch Republicans.

"Harding don't appear to make much sense," Stillman volunteered, "but ol' Cal, now, he's got my vote. He knows what the farmers want, bein' one himself."

"Yep," agreed Bert, "If the gov'ment is going to get straightened out, Cal's the man to do it. He's honest as the day is long and he don't waste words nor money. Knows the value of a dollar, he does."

And so the conversations went until the first Tuesday of November when Stillman, Bert and other men in the Hollow traveled over to Woodstock to cast their votes.

The next day's paper shouted the headline: HARDING AND VERMONT SON WIN!

And Frank turned a year older.

1922

On a steamy mid-June morning, Bessie punched down her bread dough with her right fist and swatted away a fly with her left arm.

"Too early to be this hot," she said to nobody. From the window she watched Stillman misting the raspberry bushes. Then with a sharp volley of words he handed the spray gun to Robert who had also been watching the process. Robert quickly disappeared from Bessie's view.

She decided it would be a good day to pay a visit to Hatty Ocean and bring her some rabbit stew. It would please Bobby to accompany her and play with Hatty's granddaughter, Beverly. She hurried about her duties in anticipation of her afternoon plans.

Later, she went outside to look for Robert. Suddenly a pain-filled scream pierced her ears. She darted toward the sound and discovered her son huddled against the side of the barn. Stillman was standing over him with the ox whip in his hand.

"Enough!" yelled Bessie, bending down to block her son from another lash of the whip.

"Get away, woman, or you'll be next! I told him not to fool with that spray gun! Here's a lesson he shan't forget!"

But Bessie didn't heed her husband's threat. She scooped the weak sobbing boy into her arms and, walking determinedly into the house, laid him gently on the settee. She was expecting Stillman to follow and strike her as well, but she was more consumed by her son's need than fear of her irrational husband. She removed his damp, soiled shirt and trousers and bathed his limp body with warm water and creolin disinfectant. She cooled his forehead and hummed softly until he fell asleep.

Stillman didn't come into the house until the cows were settled and supper was served. He never mentioned the incident. He just sat sourly, wolfing down biscuits and gravy. Bessie knew that even though she had been able to stop Stillman's cruelty today, it would not always be so. His fits of anger were becoming more and more intolerable.

*   *   *

Robert was approaching five and curious about everything he saw. And farm life provided much to be curious about.

He came dashing around the corner of the house one day as Bessie was weeding the garden.

"Mother, Mother!" he panted. "Come quick! Ol' Jenny had a calf inside a her and it just come out! Father had to cut it out, but ol' Jenny's all right. He wiped off the little calf 'cause it looked turrable, but then he put the baby right near Jenny's head so's she could see it. Come on, Mother!"

Bessie felt her son's excitement and let him lead her by the hand to the barn to see the grand event.

As they approached the barn, Robert continued to chatter, "Now I know you and Father was fibbin' to me about baby calves coming from the gravel pit. You was, warn't ya? "Cause Father told me Jenny swallowed some calf seeds and that's how that baby got in there!"

Bessie looked into the barn and the sight of new life warmed her heart. She saw Stillman tenderly stroking old

Jenny. He looked up at Bessie and their eyes met. He winked and sent Robert for a dipper of water.

*   *   *

When the raspberries were ripe and plentiful, Bessie set aside a day to make preserves. As she poured the melted paraffin over the hot berry mixture, a squeal came from the parlor.

She rushed in, wiping her hands on her apron, to find Robert standing near her treadle sewing machine. The index finger of his left hand was pinned down by the needle.

There was a look of fright on his face and his blue eyes were open wide. Bessie felt her own fear rise in her throat, but she moved quickly to adjust the wheel to raise the needle and release his finger.

She managed a smile and said, "Well, now we know what to do to keep you in one place for a while!"

Hot tears were streaming down Robert's cheeks and he did not smile at all. Bessie made a solution of Epsom salts and sat him down at the kitchen table to soak his finger. There he remained until she had finished her preserves.

*   *   *

Haying went on throughout the summer months. Frank and Stillman spent long, hot days in the fields cutting, tumbling, and pitching the mounds of hay into the wagon.

Bessie sighed each time she saw the oxen heading back to the barn because it meant she had to interrupt whatever she was doing to climb up into the barn loft and distribute the hay as the men forked it up to her.

On a day when the sun was straight up in the sky, Bessie knew her men would want a cool drink to accompany their lunches. She pumped some water, cold from the well, into a blue enamel pail. She added a pinch of ground ginger root and a scoopful of sugar and stirred it well with a long-handled wooden spoon. She started off toward the east field near the John lot where she knew she'd find all three of her men.

As she crossed the brook, she paused for a moment to watch how slowly the water was running. Scarcely more than a trickle at this time of year, but she loved the sound it made. She wondered how much water was flowing down below and made a mental note to take Robert there one day soon to cool himself on the rocks under the falls.

She walked on and soon spotted Stillman hoisting a bundle of hay into the wagon. The oxen stood waiting patiently nearby.

Suddenly her eyes turned toward a young beech tree where she saw her five-year-old crawling out toward the tip of an upper limb.

Bessie rushed to the tree just as Robert came crashing down to the ground with a thud. He lay unconscious for a few seconds with the breath forced out of him. Bessie took the handkerchief from her pocket, dipped it in the cool ginger water, and wiped his face and forehead as he slowly revived.

Stillman, who had heard the branch crack, dropped his pitchfork and hastened to the spot where his son lay.

"Is he all right?" he asked. Bessie could detect the fear in his voice.

"He's had a good scare, but no broken bones, I s'pect."
She was flexing Robert's shoulder, arm and knee joints,
"Probably won't do that again for a while."

Stillman's concern took the form of anger and he
berated his shaking son for damaging the limb of a healthy
tree.

*   *   *

Robert

That summer Stillman decided to buy a one pipe wood
furnace so that there would be central heating in the house.
It was a new idea that was beginning to catch on in the area.

The day of delivery arrived. A truck pulled up and two men carried all the pieces through the bulkhead into the cellar. They assembled the furnace. One of the men cut a three-foot square hole in the floor of the kitchen. Then Robert lay on the floor near the open hole, peering down into it to watch the construction process. Bessie kept a watch over her son. The final step was to cover the hole with the metal grid register.

When Frank and Alna came in from picking corn, Robert couldn't wait to show them the new addition to their home. The furnace sat that late summer through the corn and buckwheat harvest.

In October, the time came to try out the new hot air system. Stillman placed two three-foot logs nearly a foot in diameter into the firebox and lit the logs. An oil coating, used as a rust preventative, began to cause smoke. It rose up through the kitchen register and permeated the whole house. Bessie sputtered as she raced to open doors and windows. She grabbed towels and furiously fanned the smoke which became thicker before it subsided finally. The acrid smell took her breath away.

She couldn't withhold her frustration. She flung her words at Stillman as she closed the last window.

"I don't want that consarned contraption in this house! The stove's suited us just fine. Take that fool thing out of here!"

Stillman didn't answer. He went back down in the cellar to recheck the furnace.

The next morning there was no sign of smoke or odor and an even warmth was flooding the kitchen when Bessie came out of her bedroom.

"Well, what do you think of my contraption now, Mother?" he asked.

Bessie walked over to the sink and began pumping water to fill the kettle. She wouldn't give him the satisfaction of admitting she had been quick to judge and just uttered a smug, "Humph!"

1923

Winter brought three boarders back to clear lumber in the woods. Two slept upstairs next to Frank's room. The other slept in Frank's room, now shared with his brother, Robert.

Bessie had to rise an hour earlier to prepare breakfast each morning. She cooked potatoes, ham, biscuits and coffee. She made oatmeal or cornmeal mush as a sweet treat. When she baked potatoes, she would add them to the dinner pails along with a slab of cornbread and a piece of dried or smoked meat. She often slipped one or two extra potatoes into Frank's coat pockets to keep him warm while he skied his way to school.

After all the men were about their business, Bessie began straightening up the kitchen and making preparations for the evening meal. It was tiring work cooking for seven adults and one boy whose appetite was continually increasing.

In the winter, Bessie washed laundry in two washtubs—one filled with boiling water and the other with warm water for rinsing. She scrubbed the clothes with homemade lye soap using a scrub board. Her knuckles became painfully sore. Then she wrung out the heavy articles until she couldn't squeeze anymore water from them. She carried the load in a basket to the porch where she hung the clothes on lines used just in winter. The cold air froze the clothes almost as soon as she hung them. It stung her eyes so that she walked back inside blinking back tears. Before the next load was hung, she warmed her freezing, aching hands in the oven. It took the better part of the day to complete this chore.

After one wash day, Bessie was just coming from the pantry with a large jar of Harvard beets when she saw Robert come out of her bedroom where he had been napping. He stood near the hot air register intently studying something that he held in his chubby fingers. Bessie stepped into the kitchen and heard a clinking sound. She saw her son drop to the floor and peer down the opening.

"Oh, oh!" He looked up at his mother horrified. "I was just looking at your pretty ring. I didn't mean to drop it. It just slipped!"

She knew immediately that it was the gold ring with the garnet setting that Stillman had bought her at the Rutland Fair a few years back. She hurried down to the cellar with Robert close behind. Together they began searching around the furnace area with a lantern. She removed panels of the furnace and looked inside. After a while, she gave up searching. Most probably the ring landed on the firebox and was not retrievable due to the intense heat.

As they walked back upstairs, Bessie cautioned Robert not to mention the subject of the lost ring ever to Stillman.

That evening after supper, Bessie popped some corn on the parlor stove. Then she sat down at her piano to play some Irish tunes which the boarders loved to hear. The missing ring was never found nor was it ever talked about again.

*   *   *

Another wintry evening, all the men were sitting in the parlor. Stillman was busily whittling a wooden rifle for his son who was sitting cross-legged on the floor watching his father's skillful hands shape the stick of pine.

Suddenly there was a strange metallic ringing that echoed across the valley. Robert jumped. "Wha's that?"

"Oh, someone must have let that blue-whiskered tuskus out of its cage again," replied Stillman with a wink at the others.

Bessie shook her head. "That's just old Ezra Ocean going to the barn, Bobby."

Nelson Cruthe, one of the boarders, added to the explanation. "Ayuh. That Ezra works hard for a blind man. Truth is, I was there the day he got struck blind. He was bringing home a load a' lumber when a bad storm come up. Ezra, he beat them horses to git 'em movin', but they wouldn't budge. Too heavy a load for 'em. Ezra kep'a beatin' 'em knowin' the storm was brewin'. Wall, right then a bolt'a lightnin' comes down and strikes the binding chain, explodin' it into links. And one of 'em hits ol' Ezra right in the eyes."

Bessie watched Robert's eyes get larger and larger as he listened with great interest.

Nelson went on, "So Ezra's knocked flat and commences ta holler he can't see nawthin' and he's holdin' his eyes. Another fella and me, we begun ta load off the wagon quick as we could. By then we was all soaked ta the skin and thunder was crashin' all 'round us. The team was scar't and hard ta quiet down. But, by godfrey, we managed ta git ol' Ezra home. He ain't never druv a team agin. Been blind as a bat since that day."

The ringing sound echoed again. Robert's eyebrows knit together in curiosity. "But what makes that noise?"

Frank, who had been sitting silently through the conversation, shook his head slowly. He smirked at his younger brother's ignorance.

60

Another boarder, Ed, explained, "So's Ezra could find his way to the barn and privy, his son Wilbur stretched a wire like a clothesline from the main house out to the barn. He attached a metal ring with a leather strap hanging from it for Ezra to hold on to. The noise you hear is the metal ring sliding on the wire. A good distance away through these hills, it makes a screechy sound like a wounded animal, I reckon."

"And now, young man, it's bedtime for you," Bessie interjected.

"Aw, do I hafta?" Robert lamented.

Stillman snapped his fingers and pointed his right index finger at his son without a word. Robert promptly said his goodnights and made preparations for bed.

*   *   *

Tales the boarders told and Bessie's piano playing wiled away the drab January and February evenings. Alna worked on embroidery and knitted socks and mittens. Bessie pieced quilts from scraps in her rag bag and tied them by hand. Every bit of yarn, thread or fabric was used and reused. Stillman's philosophy was "make do" with what was available, and if something was wanting, make it.

Bessie admired him for his self-taught skills. Even though he had completed just three grades of formal schooling, he never stopped learning. He perused the *Vermont Standard* from front page to back, discussing national as well as local news.

She was sometimes stunned by the thought that her husband had lived forty years before she ever met him. He had left home at fifteen and worked as a farm hand, barber, mill worker, railroader, grocery clerk and carpenter. He

61

talked of helping build several houses on South Street in Woodstock. There were probably even more occupations of which Bessie was not aware.

However, his two former wives were of more interest to her than his work history. In moments when she allowed herself to daydream, she wondered what those two women looked like, what places they had lived and what their lives with Stillman had been like. She knew his second wife, Alna Baker, was buried in Quechee in a large plot that he had bought when she died. Bessie vividly remembered seeing her name on a small stone on the day her mother was buried.

Although she was curious about his other wives, Stillman never volunteered information and she dared not bring up the subject. Sometimes, however, when she was in the kitchen, she would hear him talking to the men in lower tones. She would catch a word or phrase and know he was sharing bits of his past.

In late March, Bessie watched the weary men come dragging in after a long day's work. They were carrying several pails of new sap from the sugar maples that bordered Copeland's pasture. Stillman and Nelson set the buckets on the kitchen table. Bessie peered in at the glistening wet contents.

"Trade ya this sap for some sugar on snow afta suppa," Nelson bargained.

Bessie was elated. Sap running meant spring, and just the thought of it sent warmth to her soul. "Well, I reckon that's a fair trade."

She poured all the sap into her largest kettle and placed it on the back of the stove to boil down while she served up the evening meal of ham and boiled potatoes.

After the meal, she sent Robert out with a clean bucket with instructions to pack it with fresh, clean snow from the back of the house. When the sap was properly boiled down and slightly thickened, she set it aside to cool. She called everyone in to fill a bowl with snow, then she ladled the sweet amber syrup into each bowl. The special treat was enjoyed by all. Bessie made certain that there was enough syrup left over for buckwheat cakes next morning.

Stillman did not do maple sugaring to sell, but he did tap enough trees to provide syrup for their own needs. Sometimes, when the supply didn't last until the following spring, Bessie would buy a gallon or two from neighbors with her egg money.

After the last of the wood was cut and taken out of the valley to the mills, Nelson and the others left. Bessie was happy to have just her family around again. Her work load was cut in half as well.

During the mud season of April, Stillman managed to build a second porch on the side of the house that faced the road. That pleased Bessie. She looked forward to warm days when she could sit out in a rocker and watch the road.

Once in a while now, an automobile would come chugging up the dirt road. Everyone would stop their work to stand and watch. While engine powered vehicles were becoming a common phenomenon in town, few of them ventured up the steep hills of the Hollow.

Bert Curtis had a 1907 Brush. It had the appearance of a buckboard with a one-cylinder engine attached. It couldn't climb the steeper inclines when loaded, so Bert had to get out and walk along beside it, steering to keep it on the road. Bessie heard the men refer to it as Bert's ol' putt-putt.

Ben Smith, on the farm above, had an old Model T that he drove into town on occasion. That vehicle smoked and sputtered more than Bert's. Bessie's chickens squawked and flew into the air whenever Ben came choking up or down the hill.

Stillman, Bessie feared, was not going to keep in step with the times. His oxen provided enough power for his transportation needs according to him. Frank, on the other hand, talked often of buying a car and tried his best to convince his father of the advantages.

Occasionally, vendor's wagons passed by the farms with their bells and clanging wares causing more disturbance for the inhabitants of the barnyards.

Bessie particularly awaited the Fuller Brush and the Watkins wagons. She always seemed to need a new kitchen broom from the Fuller salesman. They wore down quickly on the plank floors with tracked in mud. And the square wagon with the Watkins logo always intrigued her. There were so many containers to investigate, each one curing an ill, soothing the skin, or making life better in some way.

In the end, she always bought a pint of vanilla for flavoring, a tin of burn salve, and some liniment for the cow's udders. She was careful with her egg money and didn't want to squander it.

*   *   *

May was planting time again. Stillman needed everyone's help to set the potatoes in mounds in long rows. The work had to be done by hand and was back-breaking. A seed sower was used to plant the corn and buckwheat. This year Stillman also cultivated an acre of strawberries across the brook near the John lot.

After the fields were planted, Bessie had time to put in her own garden behind the house. She made rows of parsnips, leaf lettuce, popcorn, carrots, beans, turnips, squash, onions, peas and beets. After a long winter of eating canned foods from jars stored in the dirt cellar, she could almost taste fresh-cooked beets or leaf lettuce stacked in a bowl layered with sugar and apple cider vinegar.

It was the last day of May when she finished the last of her seed planting. Stillman and Frank had taken the team and buggy and gone to Greenbush to visit his sister Mary and her husband, Ralph Bowen. Their purpose in going was partly business – to buy a young sow – and partly for a break from planting.

Little Robert was running around making shooting noises and aiming his wooden rifle at every bird he spotted.

Bessie got up from her knees and put a hand to her back. She felt achy from her neck to her ankles, but she was relieved that the garden was in.

Suddenly she heard familiar tinkling and bleating sounds from down the road. Without even looking, she called to Robert. "Come quickly, Bobby. Mr. Copeland's coming!"

Her son came running and jumping to the edge of the road and stood motionless with his arms down at his sides, his wooden rifle dangling on one finger.

Up the road ambled Mr. Copeland. He was short, portly, and had a long reddish handlebar mustache which connected to his beard. His head was bent and his face was red from the heat. Behind and beside him shuffled about one hundred merino sheep, bleating and jingling their bells as they clambered up the incline.

The farm dog Buster came racing from the barn when he, too, heard the noise. He sat by Robert with his tail wagging vigorously.

Suddenly Buster jumped up. He spotted the golden collie that was following behind the sheep, nipping at their heels when they strayed off the road and barking authoritatively if necessary.

Buster began barking loudly in return.

"Hush, Buster! Sit!" Robert reprimanded.

Robert and Buster
Frank is in the Barn

Mr. Copeland looked up and waved. "Hullo, son. Good dog you got there. Mornin', Miz Gay. Hot day for May, ain't it!"

Bessie nodded. "Too hot for taking sheep up to pasture. Bobby," she instructed, "run to the well and get Mr. Copeland a dipper of water."

"Thank ya kindly. I had a big thirst," the sheep herder said.

Robert brought the bucket and gave the dipper to Mr. Copeland who eagerly drank down the cold water.

"See you folks in the fall."

Bessie and Robert watched the unusual parade as it passed by on its way to the pasture near the top of Long Hill.

Bessie called Robert inside for lunch. She pounded down the huge mound of dough rising on the back of the stove and pinched off a piece to hand to her son who popped it in his mouth and asked for more.

"Too much raw dough and you'll end up looking like your Uncle Will!" referring to her older brother who was on the hefty side.

She set out a pitcher of milk, a bowl and some Royal Lunch soda crackers. Robert broke up the crackers in the bowl, poured on milk and began to eat. Bessie shaped her dough and placed the oval loaves in greased tins, covered them with linen towels to await another raising. Meanwhile, she began to make oatmeal cookies.

"Well, look at that," Bessie exclaimed. "I've emptied the oatmeal box. Guess you can have it to make candy."

She put a little brown sugar in the box, dripped in a small amount of water and vanilla, and recovered the box. She handed it to Robert saying, "Now shake it a little and roll the box back and forth like this." She showed him and he began to roll the box on the table while she spooned cookie dough on the large tins.

"Now open the box and see what you have."

Robert opened the lid and found several brown sugar balls rolling around on the bottom. He picked each one out, rolled it in his fingers and popped it in his mouth.

"Tastes good like candy!" he said, licking his fingers.

Alna had taken to her bed with a fever and needed rest. Bessie decided to create a diversion for her son to keep him quiet for the afternoon. She instructed him to fill the wood box, saying as she often did, that it would help make him grow.

While he was busy, she collected two tattered sheets and a blanket. She pushed the chairs in at the table and placed the folded blanket on the floor beneath the table. She spread the sheets over the table, leaving a small opening through which a small boy could crawl.

Robert's eyes were wide with wonder as he deposited the last armload of wood in the box.

"There," Bessie said. "Now you have a tent to take your nap in. You can make believe the chair legs are trees and you are out in the woods."

Robert was visibly excited. He picked up his wooden rifle where he had placed it before lunch.

"Hafta take my gun 'case I see any bobcats." He disappeared into his makeshift tent and fell asleep with just a few murmurings to himself.

Bessie ladled some warm water from the stove's reservoir and heated it to boiling in the black kettle. Then she steeped some ginger tea and brought it in to Alna. She could smell the musterole on Alna's chest as she entered the room. Alna's eyes looked glassy and her forehead was damp with perspiration.

"I wish I could bring the cows home, Mother. I'm no help to you with Dad and Frank gone."

"Pay me no mind, dear. You just drink this tea while it's hot and get yourself well."

As she went back to her tasks, Bessie thought about her daughter. She'd finished her schooling to eighth grade and continued to live at home, working hard on the farm and for some of the neighbors. Bessie could not see a bright future for her. She wanted Alna to see more of the world than the Hollow. She knew she should be meeting eligible men and longed for her to marry a young man who would care for her and give her a good life.

Stillman required hard work from Alna. He was becoming more demanding, harsher, and found more excuses to use liquor. There were occasions when he would go to town, start drinking, and not come home until early morning. Bessie felt Alna's fears. They were fears the whole family shared. And even though Bessie depended upon Alna for help and companionship, she wanted more for her only daughter – more than she herself had had.

Duty broke into her thoughts as she realized in the absence of the men, she would have to set off after the cows and get the milking done before supper could be eaten. Robert was still sound asleep under the table.

*   *   *

At the end of the Decoration Day weekend, Frank and Stillman returned from Greenbush with news of relatives and tales of life beyond the Hollow. They had the pig, but Stillman also had a gift for Bessie, a pot with a pink fuscia plant. She was weary from work but appreciated the beautiful, bright flower.

Bessie and Alna worked with Stillman and Frank to complete the haying. When the mounded wagon was brought to the barn, Bessie climbed up into the mow and pitched the hay to the back corners. The perspiration flowed down her face and neck. The chaff stuck to her body.

The process of canning began as soon as vegetables ripened. Throughout the summer, Bessie boiled quart jars and placed them with tongs on clean towels. Then she filled jars with steaming vegetables. She set the rubber rings in place, put the glass lids on, and snapped the wire closures down to seal the contents. After allowing the jars to cool, she stored them in the root cellar of the basement. Even though the kitchen was hot and steamy, and she felt wilted, she had a sense of wellbeing knowing that there would be plenty of food in store for the hard winter.

*   *   *

Friday, August third, was another hot haying day. The wagon had been loaded to overflowing with cured hay early in the morning. Now at the barn, the men were hoisting it with long pitchforks into the mow. Bessie felt the heat more intensely near the rafters where she pushed the hay back.

By mid-afternoon, Bert Curtis chugged into the driveway. He unloaded the tall milk cans as Robert scampered up to the vehicle with Buster at his heels. Bert set the last milk can down, ruffled Robert's hair and strode through the barnyard gate.

"Hullo, Stillman . . . Frank. Heard the news? We got ourselves a new president!"

Bessie heard the voices and appeared in the doorway above.

"What's this about a new president?" she called down as she wiped her sticky forehead.

"How 'do, Missus.." Bert touched the brim of his hat as he acknowledged her. "Yep. Folks are jawin' about it all over town. Harding died out there in Californee last night. So as quick as they could, they telegraphed Bridgewater. Ol' Perkins run the news up the hill to Plymouth Notch. Woke up Cal Coolidge, he did, to tell him he's the president. His father, John, gave him the oath right there in the parlor in the middle of the night. Roads have been jammed with people runnin' up to Plymouth all mornin'. Saw ol' Doc Cram comin' back into town. He says Coolidge and the wife are on their way to Washington. Took a train over ta Rutland. Shore cut their vacation short."

"Land sakes," Bessie uttered, "a Vermont farmer for president!"

Stillman shook his head. "Sure takin' on a bushel a' troubles. Country's in a mess right now."

"Think he's the man for the job?" Bert asked.

Stillman replied, "Can't do any worse."

*   *   *

Robert had passed his sixth birthday and was old enough to start going for the cows. Bessie took him on walks to familiarize him with the trail. She used these opportunities to teach him the names of flowers, birds and trees they saw along the way.

One day they were up on the John lot, so named for a family who had owned it many years back. The only sign now of a previous life there was a cellar hole half-hidden by overgrowth.

Bessie was walking near a small stream that ran through the property. Robert trailed behind. Suddenly she saw something that startled her. Just a few feet away she spotted a strange lizard sunning itself on a rock. It was brownish-yellow and over a foot long. She had never seen anything like it. She stood motionless and called softly for her son to come quietly.

As Robert approached, he stepped on a twig. The sound alerted the creature. They both watched as the prehistoric-looking reptile slid into the stream and disappeared. Bessie wished she'd had more time to study this unusual animal before it was gone. Surely, she thought, this has been a once-in-a-lifetime experience.

By the close of summer, Bessie felt comfortable about sending her youngest child after the cows by himself.

Also by the end of summer, Alna was living in Quechee where she had taken a job doing housework. Her trips back to Curtis Hollow were infrequent because transportation was difficult and costly. She had to take a train from the station in Quechee to the depot on Pleasant Street in Woodstock. From there she needed to hire a stage into Bridgewater and walk the long way home, hoping to get a ride with a neighbor.

Bessie missed her daughter. Stillman, she feared, missed the extra hand. But Bessie was secretly happy for Alna. She thought about how much she had enjoyed living in town with the excitement of people and activity. Now, perhaps Alna would meet someone and fulfill the dreams she had for her.

*   *   *

Late one day Robert came into the kitchen holding a handful of buttercups and bluets. He had collected them while bringing home the cows.

"How pretty," Bessie remarked as he held the flowers up to her. "Let's get a glass of water for them."

Robert often picked wild flowers, especially violets in spring, and Bessie always reacted as though each flower was most precious to her. Her son was caring and had a deep love for nature. She knew that he took time to observe things.

That night at bedtime, she reminded Robert to say his prayers as she always did. As she turned to leave his room, he began to speak. "Mother, I stepped in a weasel's nest today. You shoulda seen 'em. Five, six little weasels run up my pant legs while I was standin' on a brush pile. Scar't me a little. But quick as a wink I took my pants down and brushed 'em off. They run in all directions. Guess I did, too!"

Bessie smiled and gave her son a reassuring hug. What an experience that must have been for such a young boy, she thought.

*   *   *

That September Robert started school. Bessie walked down with him on the first day and introduced him to his teacher, Luna Colston. Robert shyly clung to Bessie's skirt as he peered into the room where several scrubbed-clean children of various ages were peering back with looks of anticipation on their faces.

Bessie saw that the classroom had not changed since Alna and Frank had attended. The one-pipe woodstove still occupied a large central spot. The desks were arranged close together with the oldest students sitting in back. The few windows offered minimal light. A pendulum clock sat on a ledge on the wall. A large earthen jug filled with water for drinking and washing purposes sat by the teacher's desk. The dunce stool occupied the corner on the opposite side of the desk. The detached outhouses were situated in back of the school.

The scene reminded her of the small school she had attended so many years ago in East Barnard, and for a moment warm memories flooded over her.

Miss Colston took Robert's hand and led him to a seat in the front row. Bessie waved, turned, and walked back up the hill feeling a deep sadness that her baby was beginning a life of independence from her. How quickly the years had passed since her youngest was born, she thought.

But autumn, as other months, afforded little time for pondering. There were apples to pick, potatoes to be dug, corn to get into the barn, green tomato relish to make, squash and turnips to put in store - and more canning. The hog had already been butchered and the fat had to be rendered for soap making.

*   *   *

On a grey October day, Frank informed Stillman that one of the cows couldn't be found. She hadn't been with the rest when he had gone to bring them home.

Bessie winced as Stillman cursed and flung angry insinuations at Frank. She knew Stillman had to blame someone for the costly loss. Sometime later Frank said he heard bellowing coming from the ledges near Bert Curtis's property line.

"Dammit, Frank! Grab the rifle! We've got to find 'er before dark!"

Bessie and Robert stood rooted as the men set out to find the missing cow. Bessie shook her head. She knew it didn't bode well. There was a good chance that the cow had fallen into a crevice in the slick rock.

She noticed Robert's round eyes staring up into hers and he appeared to be trying to read her face.

"Mind you, Bobby, don't ever go up near those ledges! Ever!"

After what seemed an eternity, the piercing sound of a rifle rang out. Bessie started. Her fears had been confirmed. Soon a somber father and son returned home without the cow. No one had anything to say during supper that evening.

*   *   *

By November, Stillman had completed a new, larger storage shed. He even built a bigger chicken coop for Bessie's laying hens.

The second week of November brought deer hunters into the valley. For the two-week season, Bessie knew she could count on having company. Stillman's half-brother Idey was one who would often stay a week. He would go off hunting with Stillman and Frank from dawn to late afternoon. Bessie always packed meat and bread which they stuffed in their mackinaws, but when they arrived back at the house, cold and wary, they were starved for a hot, sumptuous meal.

At least one of the hunters would get their buck and provide venison for the winter months. The meat was frozen and left to hang from the shed rafters or packed in hay and stored in the cold shed.

Even though the work load increased somewhat, Bessie welcomed the hunters. Having the house filled with men kept Stillman more even-natured. His flare-ups were less frequent. And even when liquor was available, Stillman was less likely to inflict his behavior on his own family.

Then, too, there was the competitive story-telling each evening as the men told of the day's adventures. Bessie listened with one ear to the tales of the big buck on the ridge that was just out of rifle shot. Or the eight-pointer that was hit but bolted out of sight, never to be found. Or the "durned out-a-stater that shot ol' man Smith's jersey heifer." Some of the stories seemed to be repeated season after season. Only the names changed.

*   *   *

Thanksgiving Day was a time of feasting on venison and sometimes a turkey from the farm near the Wilbur Ocean place. Bessie spent days preparing apple, mince and pumpkin pies, a variety of vegetables and hot baked breads.

Bert Curtis, who had recently lost his father, was asked to join the family dinner and brought some of his homemade oatmeal cookies. Alden Wheeler was also a guest that year much to Bessie's delight.

During the meal, Bessie asked, "Dad, will you have some more turnips?"

Little Robert, who was seated close by, chimed in, "Want some 'tatoes, Dad?"

Alden snickered. Stillman placed his hand on Robert's shoulder and declared sternly, "I'm your Dad. He is your grandfather!"

Robert's ears turned red and he glanced quickly at his mother who gave him an approving smile.

Bert turned to Frank, seated on his right, and commented, "Well, I see you and your sister eat that venison nowadays. I recollect your father telling me there was a time you wouldn't touch the stuff with a ten-foot pole!"

Bessie smiled, "I'd forgotten that. They wouldn't eat a lick of rifle shot buck. So I'd fool 'em. I'd ask Stillman, right in front of 'em, to pick up some beef at the store in town. Then, when Frank and Alna were off to school, I'd take venison from the shed and wrap it in brown paper just like store-bought meat. They'd spy it on the shelf when they'd come home from school. They ate their venison and were none the wiser."

Alna wrinkled her brow and exclaimed, "Mother, how das't you!" But she broke out in a big grin in spite of herself.

*   *   *

Christmas came with scarcely a notice except for a little extra fuss for the main meal and some carols sung around the piano after chores were done. Bessie had knit warm socks for the men and mittens for Robert and Alna. She also had been able, with her egg money, to buy fresh oranges for all the family.

Christmas on a farm was like any other day. Cows to milk, fresh hay to lay, wood to bring in, and livestock to feed. A farm never stopped for a holiday.

Bessie wished she could celebrate Christmas at the Bridgewater Congregational Church to listen to the music and hear the message of the birth of God's Son; but on the farm in 1923 that privilege was not an option.

Throughout the white winter, Stillman felled timber and cut up logs to keep ahead of the constant need of seasoned wood for heat and cooking. The wood cut this winter couldn't be burned until the following year.

While Stillman worked diligently to supply the needs of his farm, the lumbermen worked for companies who paid Stillman and other land owners for the timber on their acreage. The logs were stacked in cord piles as measurement for payment to the farmers. The lumber was then taken out of the valley on drays, heavy sleds driven by teams of horses or oxen. This was an all winter venture from which many profited.

Stillman spent many winter evenings whittling wooden handles for axes and sledgehammers which he could sell or trade. He also made long, thick wooden forks used on wash day for stirring clothes in the iron kettles and fishing them out of the boiling water.

Bessie sometimes looked up from her needlework to study the movements of Stillman's sharp knife against the oak strips as it obeyed the coaxing of his gnarled fingers. Although he seldom mentioned it, his arthritis was becoming more visible.

One cold evening, Robert was sitting cross-legged on the floor focused on a small rock in his hand. Nelson Cruthe, who had just laid the *Vermont Standard* down in his lap, glanced at the boy and asked casually, "What ya got there, Bob?"

"A gold rock," Robert declared. "Found it up by the ol' swamp." He held it up so Nelson could get a clearer look.

"Well, it shines like gold," said Nelson, "but what you got is a rock with mica specks. Puts me in mind of the gold rush days. My old Gramp used to tell over and over 'bout how gold was discovered in Chateauguay the year my Pa was born. Eighteen and Fifty-one it was. Fella by the name a' Matthew Kennedy, fishin' out in Buffalo Brook, found a chunk. Wall, don't ya know folks from all abouts come traipsin' up to these hills lookin' to pan the streams for their fortune. Good gold it was, too. Purer than what folks was findin' in Californee. Put Chateauguay on the map, I'll tell ya. A slew a' mines up in them hills. Nawthin' left of the town today, but fools keepa lookin', hopin' to get rich."

The other men nodded. And Stillman added, "I recollect ol' Bill Dugan tellin' of a mine right here on Bald Hill."

Bessie smiled. "Well, Bobby. Don't get any ideas about taking my pie pans down to the brook to look for gold!"

Robert, who had been wide-eyed with interest, lowered his head at his mother's comment and twisted the shimmering rock in his left hand.

*   *   *

Spring returned to the valley and, with it, a myriad of new tasks. Stillman and Frank went out to fix fence on the pasture boundaries carefully setting rocks back in place along the walls to keep the cattle from straying onto neighbor's land.

Bessie was overjoyed to see the livestock, stabled up all winter, come out into the spring air for the first time. She felt she could understand what they were feeling at this 'turn out' time of year.

80

But then began the tedious and unpleasant job of removing mounds of dung from the stalls in the barn and cleaning out the hen houses. And it seemed no sooner had sugaring off been completed in April that the fields had to be plowed, fertilized, and harrowed.

On a brisk April afternoon, weary from turning over earth all morning, Bessie was taking a short rest in the rocker on the porch. She spotted plump Rozey Curtis coming up the hill pulling a brown and white Guernsey cow by a short rope. The cow plodded aimlessly along behind. When Rozey spied Bessie, he tipped his straw hat and, in his slow Vermont drawl, asked her, "Would you have a gentleman heifer I might borrow?"

Bessie grinned. It was mating season and neighbors occasionally availed themselves of each other's stock for breeding. Rozey, however, had an amusing way of asking, Bessie thought.

She pointed to the barn. "Go on up. Stillman is out there now. Just came in from the lower field. How's Marshy?"

"She's been ailin' since the winter. Rheumatiz', I 'spect. I'll tell her you was inquiring'. And I'm fit as a fiddle, 'case you was ta ask."

He walked up the driveway toward the barn leading the unsuspecting Guernsey to be bred.

*   *   *

Now that Frank was out of school, he was able to earn money working for the various logging companies while still helping his father. And methodically he worked on convincing Stillman of the need of a family car. These discussions usually took place in the evening within Bessie's hearing. She kept relatively silent on the subject except to say that she thought a car would make it easier to get out more often.

Eventually, Frank's arguments wore down Stillman's resistance and the two men went to look for a vehicle. The model they bought was one that Frank had had his eye on for some time, an older, four-passenger open Overland. And Bessie could see that her tall, reticent son could not contain the excitement on his face as he chugged into the driveway behind the wheel of the motor car on that landmark day.

For the next several days, Frank tried to teach Stillman how to drive. Even Bert came up to instruct him, but the sixty-year-old farmer had no patience with gasoline powered engines built into contraptions that sputtered, sparked and lurched without reason. And no amount of cursing or fits could convince the vehicle to behave. So Frank became the sole driver.

*   *   *

The arrival of the car proved to be timely. In late May, Robert came home with a note from Miss Colston. The note explained that Robert appeared to be having great difficulty reading his primer and copying his figures from the blackboard. The teacher also said that she had observed much squinting and would suggest his eyes be checked by a specialist.

Bessie sighed deeply as she read the words over and over. She wondered how she had missed seeing this problem in her son. However, she did recall noticing him squint when looking at small objects.

When she gave the note to Stillman to read, he smashed his fist down on the table and uttered something about the school having no business meddling in his affairs.

Bessie retrieved the note and tucked it in her apron pocket, saying nothing.

The next morning, Stillman said, "Frank, you'll have to drive us over to Rutland. Haf' to see the eye doctor for Robert. Think you can manage that?"

Bessie loved to go to Rutland, and to travel there in an automobile was a thrill she could scarcely contain. When the day arrived, she dressed her best and waved to all her neighbors as Frank drove down the Hollow Road and onto the River Road. It was a long, slow, dusty ride, but for her it was an adventure.

The first stop in the busy city was the optometrist's office. Robert's eyes were tested and a pair of thick-lensed spectacles were chosen and purchased.

Next, they ate lunch in the Chinese restaurant up over the dry goods store. This was a special treat for Bessie. The room had booths that were enclosed by white curtains. And someone served her a meal that she didn't have to cook.

Finally, they did some shopping up and down Main Street. The men drifted into the hardware shop while Bessie bought some yard goods for a new dress and several skeins of wool at the dry goods store.

All too soon the day was spent and it was time to return home. Bessie was amazed at how much quicker and smoother the trip to Rutland was now that they owned an automobile.

*   *   *

The Overland and Frank's ability to drive became Bessie's liberation. Many Sunday afternoons were spent going for rides to visit relatives. They drove to Greenbush to see Stillman's sister, Mary Bowen, and to Woodstock to visit his older sister, Alice Dana. And while in Woodstock, they saw Bessie's sisters, Lottie Churchill and Lora Brown, who had also been married to a Churchill some years back.

And now they could go to dances more often. How Bessie loved to dance. And how much more convenient it was to get there by automobile than to have to hitch up the team and ride behind their odor and dust all the way to nearby towns.

The grange hall served good meals before their dances. And Stillman, who could be contrary about many things, never had to think twice about attending. Bessie and Stillman were fine dancers. Even at sixty and with the effects of arthritis, Stillman was a much sought after partner. Nor did his wife ever sit out a dance. They participated tirelessly in all the round, square and contra dances, changing partners often. Then together they would make an impressive sight gliding fluidly across the floor during a waltz.

Frank danced with a few young ladies, but he preferred to be outside discussing cars with his friends. At sixteen, dancing was not his first love.

Robert would watch the proceedings for as long as he could, then he'd curl up on Stillman's coat on the floor behind the piano. It wouldn't be long before the sound of the music lulled him to sleep.

For Bessie, dancing was a means of sweeping away all the cares and heartaches in her life. She welcomed the music in her soul. There was a carefree buoyancy in this place that she felt nowhere else.

And so she danced until it was time to awaken Robert and leave for home.

Bessie was the only one in the valley who kept hens. She bred them, took good care of them, and had complete say over which ones she kept, cooked or sold. In either case, she did the killing and dressing off. The money she earned from the sale of eggs or hens she carefully placed in a clean tin on a shelf in the pantry, or buttery as they called it.

Into that tin, also, went money from selling some of the butter she churned. It was tedious work turning and agitating the handle of the wooden churn to turn milk into butter. After the butterfat separated from the liquids, she filled wooden molds with the creamy white butter. She wrapped the molds in waxed paper, placed them in a pail and lowered them into the well to keep cool. She used whole milk to make her butter, but for everything else, the milk was skimmed and the top cream sold separately. Cream was a saleable commodity and couldn't afford to be used unnecessarily.

When the steamy days of summer were waning and harvest was at its peak, Bessie's thoughts turned to county fairs. She counted out the coins she had saved all year and was pleased to find two dollars that she could permit herself to spend.

The Vermont State Fair was held the first week of September in Rutland. And in 1924 Frank drove Stillman, Bessie and Robert there in the Overland. Bessie noticed that Frank sat a little taller in the driver's seat as they came into the fair grounds and parked alongside the other automobiles. The oxen and horse-drawn vehicles were across the field. Bessie gave a quick look in that direction as she stepped out on the running board. She couldn't have imagined even a year ago coming to the fair in a motorcar.

Familiar sights, sounds and aromas assaulted her and she was caught up in the excitement. Frank and Stillman left to examine the latest farm equipment. From there, they would check out livestock and watch harness races while sampling food along the midway.

Bessie kept Robert by her side as they weaved through crowds of people. Part of the pleasure for her was visiting with women she hadn't seen since the previous fair. And, of course, she enjoyed Floral Hall where the ladies brought their crafts to show – quilts, rag rugs, lace doilies, tatted handkerchiefs as well as knitted and crocheted items. Bessie leisurely examined all the handiwork. She could well appreciate the hours of work and skill involved in each piece.

By the time she came to the prize flowers, jams, jellies and harvest vegetables, she sensed Robert's restlessness. Reaching into her pocket, she found a nickel and allowed him to go to the next tent for an ice cream cone. She instructed him to come right back and wait for her at the door of the hall. She continued on observing the fruits of others' labors.

Soon the smell of fried onions piqued her appetite so with Robert in tow she wound her way through the milling crowd to the grange tent where wonderful foods were being cooked and served. With a few of her coins, she bought a hot meal for the two of them and sat at a table with benches to enjoy it.

All too soon the men found her with news that it was time to head home to get the cows in. Time was always regulated by the schedule of the cattle.

*   *   *

The Windsor County fair was held the last week of September on Billing's meadow in Woodstock village. Bessie liked it even more than the Rutland fair because she was apt to see more people she knew, including some of her relatives.

Perhaps there was more up-to-date technology at Rutland's larger fair, but otherwise they were similar. Floral Hall, bingo games, livestock contests, grange dinners, the midway – all were familiar.

Bessie decided to use a little of her money to play bingo this year. She listened to the man call out numbers while keeping half an eye on people passing by the tent. Thus, she was surprised when she noticed her card was full. She quickly called out, "Beano!" and received her prize of a large kettle of spices. How pleased she was. She entrusted the burden to Robert until Frank could carry it back to the car.

Later, she treated her tired son and herself to paper sacks full of flavorful popcorn at Bingham's stand. Frank and Stillman checked out the workmanship of J.J. Nuttings exhibit of caskets.

The sound of the afternoon train whistle signaled time to leave for the farm.

The first Tuesday of November in 1924 was an impressive date for residents of Vermont. They had the privilege of voting for a presidential candidate from their own Green Mountain state.

Stillman was opposed to the recent law giving women the right to vote, but Bessie insisted that Frank drive her into Woodstock with Stillman so that she could cast her ballot for Calvin Coolidge.

"Don't know much about this Charles Dawes fellow for vice-president, but he's running with Cal and that's good enough for me!"

The following day when the Rutland Herald's bold headline announced Plymouth's own son had won the election, Bessie felt good that she'd had a part in putting him in office.

*   *   *

Alna acquired a new job at the Bridgewater woolen mill doing a phase of the work called specking. She sometimes roomed at the foot of Curtis Hill at the home of her friend, Regis Donteneault. This was a great convenience with the mill being within a very short walking distance.

Bessie saw her daughter much more often now and was content to have her closer. In their conversations, Alna often remarked about the difficulty of specking, but she was beginning to learn another process of drawing in thread to the peddles of the weaving looms. In a short time, she was given the responsibility of the new position.

*   *   *

On a beautiful autumn day in early November, Stillman and Frank went hunting. Bessie saw the look of dejection on young Robert's face as he watched them disappear into the woods. She knew he felt old enough to go with them. After all, hadn't Stillman spent much time teaching him the proper use of firearms? She handed her unhappy son a thick piece of bread slathered with butter and sprinkled liberally with sugar. She suggested he go outside to play and she went back to work.

When she checked on him later, she found him sitting on the porch steps. He was holding the crossbow that Stillman had made him. He was aiming it at the sky, then towards the woods. She recognized the arrows he had beside him. They were ribs from an old umbrella she had told him to discard days earlier. She shook her head. "He's

88

handy j'lk his father. Something's always going on in that little head of his!"

She hung some scatter rugs on the line to air. Suddenly, she heard a raucous squawking coming from the front yard. She dashed through the house and out the front door. There, she spotted Robert racing toward one of her prize laying hens. The hen was lurching and jumping with a glistening arrow sticking in its side.

Robert saw his mother and began to sob, "I didn't mean to hit her! I didn't mean to, honest!"

Bessie ran straight to the shed, grabbed the ax with one hand, then scooped up the suffering bird with the other. She took it to the chopping block and freed it from its agony. She cleaned it, plucked the feathers and took it inside to her stewpot. She didn't say anything to Robert. The look on his face spoke volumes. She could have said, "No use crying over spilt milk," like her mother had often said and she could have given him a stern reprimand which he deserved. But she knew he had suffered already from guilt and the shock of actually hitting the hen.

Stillman and Frank came home to a supper of chicken and biscuits. During the meal Stillman asked, "What did you cook a chicken for tonight?"

Bessie kept her eyes on the potatoes she was passing to Frank. "Well, I knew you two wouldn't come back with anything."

Robert buried his head in his plate. And he filled the wood box extra full that night without having to be reminded. Bessie never mentioned the incident to Stillman, but she hid the crossbow and arrows in a place her son would never find.

In 1925 Stillman constructed a new kitchen next to the original one by utilizing some of the shed space. There was a window above the sink now where Bessie could look straight out to the back yard. And he cut a large hole in the wall between the two kitchens as a pass-through for food. Bessie felt this was luxurious – somewhat like the boarding houses she knew.

But the greatest luxury that year was having a telephone installed on the front wall of the old kitchen. Now her world was opening up. She could pick up the receiver and hear the voice of Mabel the operator ask, "Number, please?" Bessie thought this was the most impressive invention. She could speak to Mabel and Mabel would connect her to anyone in the valley. She could even speak to her sisters over in Woodstock.

The telephone also proved to be an essential item to own. One day in late spring, Stillman had hitched up the oxen to the dump cart and driven up near the John lot. His purpose was to fill the cart with rocks to mend the stone wall in back of the barn. Frank was already engaged in piling up fallen stones further down the wall.

Bessie was folding bed sheets when she heard Frank's deep voice.

"Mother, come quick! Dad's had an accident!"

Bessie turned ashen not knowing what she would find, but she blindly followed Frank through the barnyard, down the path to the brook. There she saw Stillman lying still on a pile of rocks in the brook. The cart was tipped from a broken wheel and most of the rocks had fallen out. The oxen stood motionless waiting for direction. Stillman was soaking wet and moaning. As they tried to lift him, he let out a horrifying scream.   They had no recourse but to drag him step by painful step back to the house.

They managed to strip off his wet clothes and get him into bed.   Bessie went to the phone and asked Mabel to connect her with Dr. Cram.   He answered and assured her he would be up within an hour.

Meanwhile, she made some hot chamomile tea and fed Stillman sips to warm him and calm him down.

Dr. Cram examined Stillman and concluded that he had broken three ribs.   He taped him up and gave him an elixir of laudanum for pain.   There was nothing more he could do. Healing would be long and painful, he added.

Bessie nursed Stillman until he felt stronger.   She cooled his brow from the fever, administered the medicine, and bathed his bruises with comforting salve.

Even though he revived, every time he moved in a way that aggravated his injured ribs, he clutched his chest and cried out. The injury intensified the pain in his joints as well which, in turn, contributed to his frequent explosive outbursts.

He made trips up to the Smith place to drink Ben's corn liquor. And he found other places to do his drinking. He came home late at times, and some nights he didn't come home at all.

One evening, long after supper was cleared away, Stillman came staggering through the kitchen door with his arms flailing. He headed straight for Bessie, cursing and yelling.

"Where's my supper! I'll teach you to have my vittles on the table when I come home! I'm gonna thrash the living daylights outa you!"

Bessie backed away from the beating she knew was coming. But she saw Frank move swiftly from the kitchen to the milk room and return with a length of rope. Before Stillman could lay his hands on her, Frank lunged at him and managed to pull the rope around his chest. He pressed his father's face against the wall and forced his hands behind his back tying them securely together. Then he wound the rope around his legs and tied it again.

All this time Stillman thrashed and cursed, threatening to beat Frank senseless, but Frank overpowered the older man, and Frank's fear and determination made him even stronger.

Bessie looked on in horror, clutching the hem of her apron up to her face. Robert peered around the corner, eyes wide and mouth open.

Frank continued to wrestle with Stillman who was beginning to weaken. In his state of intoxication, he was no match for Frank. His head was swimming and he was in visible pain. He crumpled to the floor by the cellar door and passed out. Frank checked the knots to be certain he couldn't get loose.

Bessie saw that Frank was red-faced and shaking. She opened her mouth to speak, but Frank spoke sharply. "Leave him there! You go to bed. I'll handle him in the morning!"

Although she feared Stillman's retaliation, she was proud to see her son stand up to his father. She readily obeyed him and prepared for bed. Robert scurried back up the stairs.

Bessie arose early the next morning to find Stillman still in a deep sleep. Carefully, she untied the rope and quietly went about her morning chores. By the time the boys got up, Stillman had awoken, gone out to the privy, washed and was sitting at the table. Bessie served breakfast. The usual conversation took place. Not a word about the previous evening was spoken. Bessie noticed that Frank never glanced at his father but hurried out to lay fresh hay in the stable. As he walked through to the milk room, the rope was wound up, hanging on the door knob, and she saw him look at it out of the corner of his eye. For everyone, that was the end of the incident.

*   *   *

Wilbur and Lillian Ocean had a daughter, Beverly, who was the same age as Robert. She had long black hair and a pretty smile. She and Robert attended school together and began playing together after school.

Bessie was pleased that her Bobby had someone to spend time with besides Russell Smith who could be a troublemaker at times. So she encouraged the friendship. Once she even told her son that she could tell Beverly was his best girl. Robert's ears had turned red and he'd shaken his head in denial. Bessie had chuckled, knowing she had spoken the truth.

One day Beverly's father, Wilbur, came to Bessie with a request.

"I'd really be beholdin' to you, Bess, if you could see your way clear to stay with Mother while I'm on late shift at the mill. Mother's mind is gone and someone has to be with her all the time now. Lillian's given up teachin' but she needs her sleep. So I'm thinkin' if you were a' mind to stay after supper to midnight, Lillian could sleep durin' that time.

93

Then she'd spell you so's you could get home. I'd be payin' you for this, of course."

The Oceans had been good neighbors for years. It was Wilbur's mother, Hatty, who had been there for Bessie when Frank was born at the Dugan place. She could scarcely turn down this request now that Hatty needed help.

So for the next few months, Bessie straightened up after supper meal, put on her heavy shawl, and walked the three-quarter mile path through the trees and fields to the Ocean house.

The first night, Robert insisted on going along and pleaded with her to take a butcher knife just in case she needed to protect herself from Hatty. Bessie smiled, "I don't think we'll be needing any knife, but I'd appreciate the escort from someone as strong and brave as you."

Bessie enjoyed the time she spent at the Oceans. Hatty, it appeared, needed protection from herself. She was liable to wander out of the house into the woods or harm herself touching the stoves and lamps. She rambled incoherently and dozed off frequently. Her behavior was erratic and she had to be watched carefully. But Bessie was able to get some needlework done during quiet times. Often she sang or hummed and Hatty seemed to be calmed and soothed by the sound of her voice. Though Hatty didn't appear to recognize her long-time neighbor, there did seem to be a far-away familiarity and quietness of spirit as she watched Bessie sing and crochet.

The difficult part of the evening was walking home past midnight. Only her lantern lit up the blackness of the night. And that only a very small spot in the vastness. And the sounds! The frightfully eerie sounds of creatures who could be heard just in the darkest hours. Her hope every night was that she wouldn't encounter any of the larger ones or step on any of the slithery ones.

Wilbur finally was moved to a day shift and Bessie's job was curtailed.

*   *   *

About this time, Alna began to talk to Bessie about a gentleman she had met at the mill. His name was Nelson Swanson, son of Charles and Augusta Swanson, who were born in Sweden and now lived on the Westerdale Road in West Woodstock. Nelson was of average height, very slender and had light hair and eyes. He had served in the Navy during the war and had come home to work at the mill as a weaver.

Alna confided to her mother how she and Nelson had spoken to each other on a few occasions. Then he had asked her to go for a ride and to a picture show.

Bessie saw the excitement in Alna's eyes as she talked on about this man with whom she seemed so enamored. There was an age difference between them – Nelson was thirty-two and Alna was not quite nineteen. But Bessie knew she was hardly one to mention age to Alna with her own span of twenty-seven years between her and Stillman. Alna was happy and that was all that mattered.

*   *   *

The first of July, Frank brought home the mail with a letter from Pompano, Florida for Stillman. His boyhood friend, George Buck, was coming back to the valley for a visit and wanted to stay at the farm for a while.

95

When Stillman read the letter to her, Bessie reacted to the news. "Is that old bird coming here again?"

She had tried to like George, but he had an attitude she couldn't abide. However, she silently vowed to be neighborly if not truly congenial.

Fortunately, George's visit passed quickly because summer was always a busy time. George spent his days combing the nearby woods for saplings out of which he could carve wooden canes.

Stillman went with him on one excursion. They traveled up the road past Lake Mecawee to the Dugan place and beyond to where only the cellar hole remained of the Buck homestead. Bessie listened later as the two men recounted memories of their younger days living on adjacent farms in Reading. George peeled, whittled, smoothed and stained his canes while they reminisced.

Bessie listened, also, to George criticize Stillman's way of life even as a guest in his home. She wondered why her often times harsh husband would tolerate George's comments.

"Bout time you bought a couple horses! 'Twould make your life a heap easier. You need to catch up to the times, my man. You're still livin' in the past!"

And another time, "In Florida life is a good deal better then you have it up in these hills. Don't know why you keep puttin' up with those hard winters what with your rheumatiz and all. You could be livin' like a king down where I am. I was smart to make the move when I did. Can't see why you don't."

To which Stillman only replied, "Being a Vermonter, George, is uphill livin' most of the way, but it's home."

One morning at breakfast, as he poured fresh skimmed milk into his coffee cup, George berated Stillman. "What's this! You can't even spare cream for coffee? Don't those cows of yours give cream anymore?"

Bessie waited for Stillman to explode, but instead he looked calmly at his friend and replied, "George, you been out of the Hollow too long. Can't waste cream at the table when it brings in good cash."

Bessie felt great relief the day George packed his belongings, including all the canes he'd made to sell on the train, and left for Pompano. Wherever that is, she smirked.

*   *   *

On July seventeen, Bessie wrote down a poem on a small square of note paper:

> "Flowers in the Valley may wither,
> Trees in the forest decay,
> But a mother's love lasts forever
> When all other things fade away."
> Mother

She dated it in the left corner and placed a sticker of purple violets in the right corner. When Sunday dinner was over and she and Alna were in the kitchen, she quietly presented her little gift. Alna was very moved. And Bessie was content that her daughter seemed to glow with happiness. Keeping company with Mr. Swanson was good for her.

*   *   *

Alden Wheeler spent part of the summer at the farm that year. He was retired from Dewey's Mill now. At seventy-two, he was showing obvious signs of aging. There was hardly anything left of his silky, fine reddish hair. His shoulders stooped and he moved even slower than he always had. Eight years of being widowed had taken its toll, but, to Bessie's delight, the twinkle in his eye was still evident. She felt happy and safe with her father in her house.

Alden helped Bessie pull clothes off the line, feed the animals, and milk the cows when Stillman wasn't there. He shaped biscuits, shelled peas, and brought vegetables in from the garden. He husked popcorn and scraped kernels off the cobs. And, although these tasks were time saving for Bessie, what she appreciated most was his being around talking and smiling.

It was good for Robert, too, to get to know his grandfather better. Being the youngest, he had little knowledge of his grandparents and Bessie regretted that.

She watched as Robert studied her father's gestures, especially the way his hands had begun to shake.

One morning, Robert was getting ready to eat his oatmeal and, as usual, prepared to cover it with sugar. Then he looked at his grandfather sitting beside him and glanced at his shaking hands. Bessie could almost see the wheels turning in her son's head.

"Grandfather, would you put the sugar on my cereal?" he asked.

Alden scooped a large spoonful from the bowl to oblige him and with a trembling hand, dumped the sugar in one spot on top of the cereal. "There you go, Bobby."

Robert stared at the little pile on his oatmeal, then glanced up at his mother who was forcing back a giggle. His plan hadn't worked.

A few days before Alden left the farm, he was beginning to look scraggly.

Robert overheard him say to Bessie, "Guess I need a shave." He ran the back of his hand up the side of his face.

Bessie smiled, "Yes, I'd say so. You could stash a day's worth of vittles in that beard!"

Robert piped up, "I'll shave you, Grandfather."

"Think you could do the job, Bobby?" Alden inquired.

"Shore!" Robert ran upstairs and returned with Frank's razor. With some soap in a pan of water he pumped from the sink, he lathered up Alden's face just the way he had seen Frank perform the task. Bessie watched with interest while she sat at the table removing kerosene soot from lamp chimneys.

She watched Robert guide the sharp blade down her father's cheeks, and although Robert's hand jerked a little, Alden sat patiently not saying a word. She remembered Stillman talking about his days of barbering. Maybe Bobby has some of Stillman's finer traits, she mused.

Robert finished the job leaving a few red scratches on Alden's cheeks and neck. He took them back home to Quechee as souvenirs of his visit.

*   *   *

Summer passed quickly into autumn. In every direction for a short time, the Hollow was ablaze with color.

Then, the leaves fell, sometimes coming down like a storm of colored snow and other times floating silently downward, one by one. Bessie never tired of shuffling through them and hearing the crunch beneath her feet. She inhaled the scent of fall. Dry leaves, fallen apples, chimney smoke.

She knew October was well under way when she heard the commotion of Mr. Copeland bringing his sheep down from their grazing on Long Hill. Everything about farm life had a time table.

* * *

Robert burst into the house after school one day with news. Bessie sliced off a thick piece of bread just out of the oven, spread it with sugar and butter, and handed it to her excited son. "What's the news, Bobby?"

"Miss Colston says we're gonna put on a play. And I hafta' be an Indian and dress up and all. And it's to be over at the big school in Woodstock." He bit off a big chunk of bread before continuing.

Bessie said, "Well, I guess we'll have to see about fixing you up a costume. Should be something around the house that we could use."

For the next several days Bessie thought about how she could transform her son into a realistic looking native. On one of her trips to sell eggs, she stopped at the turkey farm beyond Wilbur Ocean's place and collected a half dozen large white feathers. That afternoon she gave Robert an assignment.

"Fetch your water colors and paint these feathers nice and bright; anything but brown or black."

After they were painted, she laid them on newspaper to dry overnight. The next day she sewed them to a band of wide elastic. Robert stood rigidly as she measured the band to his forehead.

Another day she searched her ragbag and discovered a little less than a yard of burnt orange wool. She asked Robert to bring her his khaki pants and measured the length of them. She cut strips form the orange fabric, folded them, and sewed them along the sides of the pants. She cut crosswise slits down both sides, then cut up the fold, making the appearance of a fringe. Robert watched with wide-eyed interest the transformation of his play trousers.

Upstairs in an old trunk she found an old army coat which she cut into a rectangle. In the center of the rectangle, she cut a circle large enough to fit Robert's head. With narrow strips of the orange, she laced up the sides, leaving room for arm holes. This formed a vest onto which she sewed more strips of fringe to the shoulders and bottom edge.

Now Robert's costume was complete. Day after day he reported the progress of the play to Bessie. Finally, the big event arrived. Frank drove them all down to Woodstock High School.

Bessie couldn't have been more proud of her youngest child. He spoke his rhyming lines perfectly as the class performed the story of the first Thanksgiving. There were Pilgrims and Indians of various shapes and sizes shuffling awkwardly back and forth upon the stage, repeating their much rehearsed lines.

When the performance was over, all the boys bowed from the waist and the girls curtsied. Miss Colston thanked the families for coming. Then Robert found his way through the crowded hall to his parents and brother who were waiting near the main entrance.

Stillman gave his son a pat on the back and said, "Get out to the car. It's a long drive home."

Bessie smiled reassuringly and proclaimed, "You were the best dressed Indian in the play, and the handsomest, I do believe!"

Robert wore his costume daily after school. His friend, Russell Smith, played with him as they chased one another with their wooden rifles. It seemed to Bessie that she was mending a part of that costume every other day.

*　　*　　*

Near the close of deer season, on a cold November evening, the telephone rang. Bessie put the receiver to her ear and heard Matty Smith's voice on the other end. She sounded upset.

"Bess, have you seen anything of Ben's father? He went out huntin' this forenoon and never come back!"

Bessie said she hadn't seen or heard from him. Matty went on, "I've rung up everyone in the valley and nobody's seen hide nor hair of 'im. Not like him to miss the supper meal and be gone out afta' dark. He'll catch his death out there in this cold. Ben and Russell are out lookin' for him. Some of the others – Wilbur, Bert, even Rozey are searchin' around."

Bessie listened and reassured her neighbor. "I'll get Stillman and Frank out looking. Couldn't be gone too far. Don't you worry, Matty. Somebody'll find him."

As soon as she hung up the phone, she yelled for the men who were in the shed separating the day's milk.

Frank closed up the separator can, Stillman grabbed two lanterns and they headed out into the night to search for the old, bewhiskered neighbor.

Bessie went back to the kitchen to wash the rest of the dishes. She set the table for breakfast and waited.

In less than two hours the men came back, stomping the damp leaves off their boots as they stepped through the door.

They were grinning at each other, shaking their heads.

"Crazy old man!" Stillman exclaimed.

"What happened?" Bessie asked. Did you find him?"

"We found him alright! Way up near the top of Long Hill," Frank said.

Stillman continued. "We was all out lookin' and Wilbur, he spies some smoke comin' from up the hill. We all traipse up there, and there he is. Settin' in the dark with his back propped against the stone wall, warmin' his hands over the fire he'd built. He looks up at all of us and says, "Hullo.' Then Ben says, 'What are you doin' up here, Pa?'

"Then ol' man Smith says, 'Jest a settin', keeping' warm. Huntin' warn't no good. H'ain't seen a thing. Musta' fell asleep while the sun was still up.'

"Ben was a might testy by now, so he says to come on home before he freezes up there and so's these fellas can get back to their chores. Then ol' man Smith says, sober as you please, 'Don't know why you're all upset. Can't a man jest set a spell?'"

"They'll have to keep a watch on that one from now on," Stillman snorted.

"Well, at least he's home safe. No tellin' what could have happened to him out there in the dark," Bessie replied.

In early February, a heavy snow with high winds fell upon the valley. Lumbering was curtailed temporarily, and few people moved about except to carry out the chores on their own farms. Bert Curtis worked laboriously packing and rolling the road down to Bridgewater.

Then, in mid-March, another severe storm dropped three feet of new snow. That, with heavy drifting, once again isolated the valley residents.

After more packing, Bert was able to get to the general store across the bridge and bring newspapers back up the hill to people awaiting word from the outside world.

Stillman poured over the *Vermont Standard* and *Rutland Herald* as Bessie put dried dishes in the cupboard.

"Says here," read Stillman, "that ol' Colonel Coolidge died on the eighteenth of this month. Seems Doc Cram got a hold of Cal down to Washington to let him know that the ol' man was near death, but, with the storm and all, he and the misses didn't get up here 'til it was too late."

Bessie shook her head with feeling. "My, how sad."

Stillman continued, "Must've been some procession. Had to switch from train to cars in Woodstock. Says they rounded up all the buffalo robes they could to keep the whole party warm. And stopped again in Bridgewater Four Corners to warm up. From there, it says, only horses and sleighs could make it up the hill into Plymouth. Took some doin', accordin' to reports, to get those roads cleared—big bunch a' men goin' at it with picks and shovels. Axes, too. Must've been some sight."

"The president and his father were close, it seems," commented Bessie. "Must've hit Cal hard not to make it in time. I heard tell that Cal had a telephone put in the father's place. Imagine! That must have cost something to call down to Washington."

*   *   *

The calendar proclaimed that spring had arrived but snow still covered the ground.

Robert was still able to glide down the hill to school on his sled. Bessie watched him go from her window in the kitchen. She smiled. Someday he's going to slide right past that school house, she said to herself.

There was a knock on the front door. As she opened it, a stiff wind blew in. A tall, thin man stood on the step. He tipped his hat and nodded.

"Mornin', Ma'm. Name's Tom Birmingham. Mr. Gay about?

"Come in. Come in," Bessie ordered. "Pretty nippy out this morning. I'll fetch Stillman."

In a short while, Stillman came in from the wagon shed, Bessie followed behind. Tom Birmingham thrust out his right hand to Stillman. Stillman wiped his grease-stained hand on his mackinaw and returned the gesture.

"Heard you was in the valley, Mr. Birmingham. What can I do for you?"

"Well, then, you probably heard, too, I've been buying up spruce acreage from Wilbur Ocean's place up through the Hollow. Spruce is the main source of pulp, and the International Paper Company down there in Massachusetts will take all the spruce I can ship 'em. We'll send the logs all down by water – from the brook here to the Ottaquechee River, then on to the Connecticut River where they'll be hauled out at the mill. I'm here to offer money for the spruce on your land. And, it'll provide good paying jobs for the men of this valley. Would you be interested?"

Stillman agreed readily and, after some discussion at the kitchen table, the two men set about working on a price for the timber.

The arrival of Tom Birmingham and his company created more than a mild stir among area residents. The women spent their spare time talking on the telephone about the Birmingham enterprise. The company bought up property above the Smith place and began to set up camp. A crib dam was constructed a half mile up to control the flow of the brook.

And men poured into the valley. Bessie heard the sound of saws and falling timber from early morning to late afternoon. Frank began to work for the company. He cut off branches and stripped the bark. Other men in the crew cut the trunks into four-foot logs and stacked them in cord piles to be sent down river. Within a few weeks, Frank told Bessie he had quit.

"I can't hardly get this spruce pitch offa me. It sticks onto everything like glue – on my hands, my clothes, and even in my hair. The money ain't worth the aggravation! I'll work on anything but that spruce!"

After some warming rain in April, the thaw began. The sudden freshet brought the brook to life, splashing, gurgling, falling over ice chunks in its excitement and haste to join the mighty Ottaquechee. The sound of crackling ice and rushing water was heard for miles around.

The dam upstream was released and Bessie listened to the slam and bang of logs hurtling down the high water path. Stillman often came in to report on the progress and sometimes described a jam downstream. When that happened, a hoist was utilized to raise the entangled logs and reset them on their way.

Bessie could sense a spark of energy and vigor as Stillman talked of the project.

"If it weren't for these ribs and the blamed arthritis, I'd be out there forkin' those logs outa the brook. Good work for a man."

*   *   *

In June, after the winter boarders were gone, another visitor came to stay a few days. His name was Ed and he was the son of one of Stillman's relatives. Bessie didn't like him. There was something questionable about him. And to have him in her house did not set well with her.

He brought a young woman with him. "This is Billie, my squaw," he told them by way of introduction.

Bessie gazed at the thin, high-cheeked lady with the long, straight black hair. In her stylish, tight-fitting, calf-length dress and high-heeled shoes, Bessie thought she looked like she belonged on one of the pages of the Sears and Roebuck catalog. But there was a hardness in her features.

Bessie caught glimpses of the hands of the two visitors. From their scrubbed, white fingernails she knew that no hard work had marred the condition of those hands. She resented this pair. They didn't offer to help with work but ate heartily and sat around.

In two days, they drove away in their nearly-new black Studebaker with money that Stillman had loaned them.

Bessie steamed on the inside and hoped the money would be returned.

The following day, Ed returned and stayed until he received a call from Billie to come for her. And then they were back again, blowing up dust as they roared into the driveway. Ed paid back the loan, stayed another day, and they were gone again. Bessie was left with unanswered questions and extra work. This happened once a month during that summer, each time with the same order of events.

Sometimes Bessie overheard Ed telling the men he needed a fast car in his business.

"Once, up near the border, when I was transporting my goods, I was pulled over by two agents, and I tried to outrun 'em, but they . . ." Here Ed's voice lowered to a volume Bessie couldn't hear from the kitchen. However, she heard the laughter that erupted shortly after.

So that's what he's up to, she thought. He's a fool bootlegger! And this woman, she must be some sort of set up for him to use. Why else would she always look like she was out for a good time.

She didn't understand it all, but she knew she didn't like it. And she didn't like the looks Stillman gave Billie, or the coy way Billie flickered her artificial eyelashes and giggled at Stillman's attempts to be amusing.

One afternoon in August, Bessie returned to her kitchen after forking hay all day. She washed her hands in the cold water from the sink pump and splashed some on her perspiring forehead and cheeks. She lit the wood in the stove and began to prepare for the supper meal of pea soup and Johnny cake.

109

Ed and Billie had been out walking and came back with a half pail of blackberries, pleased with the meager offering. Just as if they'd done a hard day's work, Bessie muttered to herself.

Supper over and table cleared, Bessie stepped out on the porch where a slight breeze cut through the oppressive heat. She wiped her forehead and looked off toward the west. The sun was just sliding down behind Richmond Hill. She stood for a while watching and listening to the sounds of evening. She was glad the day was over. Her back, her legs, her arms, ached. Maybe she'd put some liniment on these sore muscles before bed, she thought.

She stepped back into the front room where Ed was dozing in the Morris chair with a newspaper in his lap. She heard muffled laughter coming from the back bedroom and when she approached the doorway, she saw Stillman and Billie standing close together inside the room.

"Oh, Bessie, there you are! We missed you," cooed Billie. "You should have heard the story Stillman just told me. My, it was humorous!"

Stillman stood awkwardly nodding. Bessie bristled.

"You get out of this house! And take your friend, Ed, with you! I don't care if he _is_ some sort of relative, I'll not have you here anymore!"

Stillman left the room, glaring at his angry wife. Billie darted into the front room and whined to a startled Ed.

"Pack up, Ed! We're leaving! We're not wanted here. Some relations you have, I swear!"

Ed picked up the paper that had fallen out of his lap and jumped up. "What happened?"

"Just get moving, Ed!" Billie squealed.

*   *   *

Later, Bessie was lying awake in bed beside her snoring husband. She couldn't sleep thinking about what had happened earlier. Her body was rigid. Her thoughts tumbled over themselves. Perhaps she should have handled the situation differently. Maybe she should have ignored what she saw, or waited until morning. . .. Maybe she judged too quickly and too harshly or. . .. No! She'd had enough of those two. And that fact that Stillman didn't react in any way made her wonder what else had gone on that she didn't know about.

*   *   *

After the fall fairs in September, Bessie began looking forward to the Old Time Ball held in Reading in mid-October. It was the most elegant of all the local dances. Not only did Bessie dwell on it for weeks in advance, but for long afterward as well. It was the costliest of dances, too, but the money was saved up in the egg money tin. This dance was worth a portion of her savings.

When the long-awaited evening arrived, she quit her chores early and took extra time getting ready. She put on her black dress with lace at the collar and wrists. She noticed it seemed more snug-fitting than last year but she still felt good in it.

When she came out of the bedroom, Frank and Stillman were already washed, dressed up and ready to go. Robert, too, but the scowl on his face betrayed his feelings. He was obviously reluctant to attend this dress-up affair for adults.

"Well, Bobby, are you going to dance with me tonight? Bessie asked.

"I don't want to dance with fat women," Robert blurted out.

Bessie was stricken but said nothing. She saw the look on her son's face and knew he regretted his brash statement.

"Come now," she said. "Let's get a move on before the turkey dinner is all gone."

It was a clear night with a bright moon, and Frank drove the Overland easily over the dry roads to Reading.

After the dinner and pies were consumed, Bessie and Stillman joined other pairs to form the grand march. That was followed by round and square dances, as well as the Virginia Reel and other favorites.

Frank stood on the sidelines, watching the festivities and talking to two other young men. Occasionally, he entered into a square dance. Bessie surmised that her tall, gangly son didn't possess the grace and form of his father. He was rather awkward in social settings. She hoped he would meet a girl who would appreciate him for all the attributes he did possess. He was genuine, reticent, protective, kind and industrious. She knew he would make a fine husband for the right woman.

Part way through the evening, Bessie could see Robert sitting in a corner with his head drooping. She led him outside and bedded him down in the back seat of the car, covering him with a heavy robe.

She returned to dance and socialize with neighbors and townspeople she seldom had a chance to see. The evening flew by all too quickly and all the enchantment turned again to reality.

The following day, rain poured down from morning until night without let up. Bessie sat with her mending basket, sewing a patch in the knee of Robert's bib overalls.

Robert came into the room with a furrowed brow. "I can't find my Indian pants. Do you know where they are?"

Bessie looked up. "Well, the other day a lady and a boy about your size came by. My, they were poor – dressed all in rags, holes in their shoes. So I gave that little boy your pants and was he ever happy. Doesn't that make you feel happy, too?"

Robert looked glum. "Guess so."

Bessie realized she shouldn't have told him such a yarn, but how could she make him understand the pants were threadbare and had to be thrown out. Someday he'd find out the truth just as he'd finally learned that baby cows didn't really come from the gravel pit or calf seeds.

*   *   *

In late December, Alna announced that Nelson had been offered a job in Shrewsbury, Massachusetts as an overseer on Chamberlin's dairy farm. And, since the mill was slow, Nelson agreed to take the job. Marriage was decided upon and was to take place two days before Christmas so that the couple could move quickly to Shrewsbury before the new year.

The marriage plan was not a shock to Bessie. The two had been keeping company for over a year. But moving all the way to someplace in Massachusetts was another matter. She could not sleep all that night thinking of her daughter leaving. Yes, she wanted Alna to be happy and have a good life, but did she have to go so far away to accomplish it? She began to pray and finally fell asleep shortly before the rooster began to crow.

*   *   *

Alna insisted on taking some photographs with her new Brownie box camera. She coerced her parents to run outside on the snow packed ground and pose for a picture. Bessie fussed that she looked a fright and didn't have time to remove her apron. Stillman, rising to the occasion, donned his stovepipe hat. He put one hand on his hip and the other around Bessie's shoulder. With the bare trees and mountains as a backdrop, Alna quickly snapped the picture.

"Now I'll have something to remember you by when I'm gone," she said.

Bessie and Stillman

When December twenty-third arrived, Bessie had a serious flu. Her stomach was queasy, she felt hot and cold alternately, her head swam, and she had a deep cough. She couldn't remember feeling worse – and of all days to be ill.

She watched Alna dress in her new navy blue linen with a crocheted lace collar. She thought her daughter had never looked lovelier. But this wasn't what she had dreamed of for Alna. Her dream was of a church wedding and a reception at home afterward. However, this was Alna's life and what she chose. So, she wished her well, pleaded with her to write often, and let her go.

Frank drove Alna, Stillman and Robert to Westerdale Road where they picked up Nelson and went on to Woodstock. The marriage took place in the parsonage of the Congregational Church.

Bessie was devastated that she couldn't be with her daughter. The tears streaming down her face made her head feel worse. She went into her room and fell down on the bed, covering up with a thick quilt to quiet the chills and shaking.

1927

Alna's first letter came in mid-January. The couple had arrived safely in Shrewsbury and set up housekeeping on the dairy farm. Nelson began his duties right away, and Alna soon started working for Mrs. Chamberlin. They were already attending church. By the second and third letters, Alna wrote of going to grange meetings and teaching Sunday school. The news sounded encouraging, even uplifting.

Though Bessie missed her, she couldn't help but feel joy for her daughter who had now come into her own. Perhaps in the summer Bessie could persuade Frank to drive them all down to visit the newly-weds. She kept that idea uppermost in her mind throughout the winter months.

*   *   *

Bessie removed her rabbit pies from the hot oven. She poked the golden brown crusts to make certain they were cooked all the way through. She placed the smaller pie in a basket and covered it with a linen towel.

She wiped her floury hands on her apron and slipped on her heavy sweater. She hurried through the back walkway to the shed, shivering as she went.

Stillman was hunched over the grindstone sharpening a saw blade while Robert stood by, turning the hand crank. The faster the boy turned the wheel, the faster the grindstone turned.

"Bobby," Bessie called, "When you're finished helping your father, I want you to run a pie down to Bert's. The walk will be good for you."

Stillman added, "And be sure to tell him I've got his deer hide ready whenever he's a mind to come after it."

Bessie went back to her warm kitchen after collecting the eggs. In the distance she heard the thud, thud of axes gouging away at the icy spruce trunks. Work continued daily on the Birmingham lumber project.

She noticed her son take his jack jumper out of the shed and head toward the house. The short, wide ski with the box seat over it was one of his favorite means of gliding downhill over packed snow. However, it was quite dangerous and offered little control. She had seen him take spills more times than she wanted to remember.

"Oh, no you don't!" yelled out Bessie. "You're not riding that contraption down to Bert's this time! You'll go head-over-kittle-bail and my rabbit pie along with you! Bert'll want that pie in one piece, and I'd like you that way, too, if you don't mind!"

Gloomily, Robert left the jack jumper by the steps, took the basket of steaming pie and trudged off downhill.

He was gone quite some time and when he returned, Bessie noticed he was in a lighter mood.

"Did you give Bert Dad's message?" Bessie asked.

"Yup."

"Did he appreciate the pie?"

"Yup. Said 'much obliged.' Tried to git me to eat some of his ol' oatmeal cookies but I said 'might spoil my supper."

"Well, eat up then. I saved your vittles for you."

Stillman, Frank and the boarders had already left the table.

"Bert 'llowed me to play his fiddle," Robert volunteered with his face brightening. "Showed me where to put my fingers on the neck and how to hold the bow. Taught me 'Home Sweet Home,' he did. Said I had a good ear."

"Well, you come by it naturally, Bobby. Your Grandmother Wheeler's side were all musical. And your father's a good hand at playing instruments. He taught himself, don't you know."

"When I grow up I'm gonna learn how, if I get a fiddle," Robert vowed.

"We'll see. Right now finish up and go fill the wood box. It'll help you grow."

Out of the corner of her eye, Bessie watched Robert measure himself against the nick on the door casing as he often did on his way to the wood shed.

Bessie was pleased that her son had an interest in music. That evening when she sat down at the piano, she included "Home Sweet Home" among the other songs she played.

*   *   *

Before spring vacation, a notice came home with Robert that there would be some remodeling done on his school to meet higher standards. New windows, inside toilets and an updated heating system were planned.

Stillman read the notice and remarked, "I wonder what they'll be doing with the old double privy? I could use the lumber as well as the next person. Think I'll inquire."

After a few days, Stillman yoked up the oxen to the stone boat, a heavy sled with runners and cross planks. Robert went along with him. Bessie watched as the off and nigh oxen pulled Stillman and Robert around the corner. Stillman yelled, "Gee!" and cracked the whip. The team turned right and disappeared down the hill.

Hours later the men returned walking with a heavy load stop the stone boat. Stillman had sawed the whole privy in half, bringing home the girl's side because it was in better condition.

Frank, Robert and Nelson Cruthe helped Stillman unload the half privy. Then Frank lifted the yoke over the horns of the nigh ox and returned him to the stall. Next he unpinned the bow under the off ox's neck and lifted the eighty-pound yoke from the waiting animal. After throwing the heavy yoke on the wall, he led the off ox back to his stall as well.

In the days that followed, Bessie and Frank helped Stillman affix the new privy to the outside of the back wall of the wagon shed. He cut a door on the inside wall on the walkway, making this facility about fifty feet closer to the house – a definite convenience for everyone.

Part way through the construction project, Stillman decided to go back and retrieve the boy's side of the outhouse. That half, he attached to the back side of the hay barn.

"There!" he bragged. "Three privies, no waiting! Only one in the Hollow who can claim that!"

*　　　*　　　*

In late May, Robert brought a book home from school to show his mother.

"It's a bird book. I won it in the contest," he exclaimed. "I brought in the most different flowers and I knew 'em all. Teacher says I did good."

"Well, that's quite an accomplishment. Seems to me you won last year, too."

"Yup, I did."

Frank and Stillman came in the kitchen, washed in the sink and sat down at the table still carrying on the conversation in which they had been engaged.

"'Spirit of St. Louis' he calls it. Must be some aeroplane can fly that far without stoppin'," Frank said.

"Fella's a colonel and only twenty-five years old. Airmail pilot, paper says."

"Won that twenty-five-thousand-dollar prize, too. What do you suppose anyone would do with all that money?"

Bessie interrupted, "What are you two talking about? What fella?"

"Charles Lindbergh," Stillman explained. "He just flew from New York to France non-stop the twenty-first. Set a new record. They call him Lucky Lindy."

"Imagine that!" Bessie shook her head. "Guess he is lucky he didn't fall in that big ocean!"

*　　　*　　　*

On Sunday, Bert came for dinner. Bessie served up a boiled ham meal. Conversation centered around the renovations at the school, the prospects of a good corn and potato crop, and the Lindbergh flight.

"Paper said over thirty-six hundred miles from New York to Paris. That's a lot of ocean," commented Bert.

"How could a body abide being in the air for thirty-three hours?" added Frank. "That's a whole day and a half almost."

"They got airmail all across the country now. Wager it won't be long before they're taking passengers up in the air."

"I'd give 'em 'nother ten, twenty years," reasoned Stillman. "Hafta get the kinks out first, I 'magine."

"Well, you wouldn't catch me up in one of those tin contraptions. Dangerous enough down here on terra firma," Bessie said. "I'll take my chances behind a team of oxen, even if they are slower'n cold molasses runnin' uphill in January!"

"Don't imagine any of us from the Hollow will ever be ridin' up in the air, Bess. Got enough to do to make a livin' right here," Bert added.

And from Stillman, "Ayuh, uphill livin' all the way in V'mont."

*   *   *

By the end of July, Stillman decided he needed a break from haying. He enlisted Frank to drive them all to Woodstock on a Sunday for, as he put it, a couple of dooryard calls.

The first stop was the Chrysler garage near the covered bridge on River Street. Bessie's oldest sister, Lora, lived in a tenement next door. While Bessie visited with her tall, thin sister and her three children, Stillman, Frank and Robert browsed about the garage, looking at used cars and comparing them to what they were driving.

Later, they drove into the gravel driveway of Lottie Churchill and Frank gave a squeeze on the horn. In seconds, Bessie's shorter, stockier sister came scrambling out of her house and embraced Bessie.

"Nobody's home but me. Come in, come in. House is a mess. Wa'nt expecting comp'ny. My how you've grown, Bobby. Frank, I declare, you get any taller, you'll have to stoop goin' through the doorway. Stillman, how's the arthritis?" Lottie scarcely took a breath as she responded to everyone at once. They followed her into the house.

"Coffee pot's on the stove. I 'magine you'll be havin' some cold milk, Bobby, with a piece of that berry pie on the sill. Sit down. Sit down."

Bessie was delighted to be in her sister's kitchen. It was warm and inviting. Now that telephones were installed, they were able to talk more often, but nothing replaced being together and enjoying a chat over coffee.

The men devoured their pie and went outside to walk around. Bessie and Lottie continued their conversation. Bessie couldn't help but wonder what it would be like to live as her sisters did in houses with no livestock, no hayfields, no winter boarders. Just a yard, a garden and the pleasure of residing in the village.

For the last stop, Frank drove to the top of Breezy Hill in Prosper, just north of Woodstock village. Bessie savored the joy of driving through the two musty covered bridges along the way.

The hilltop home of her brothers was a very desirous parcel of land and further from neighbors than any in Curtis Hollow. Acres of apple trees dotted the hillside. Bessie took in the spectacular view down into the valley. It seemed she was on top of the world.

The house for the two bachelors was rustic and austere. Cats, at least a dozen of them, strutted and stalked around the grounds. One cow in the barn provided the milk and butter the two men needed. Bessie smiled as she spotted the gravestone in the front yard. It marked the place where a huge maple tree, severely damaged by lightening, had once stood.

Perly, thin and balding on top, and Will, also balding but shorter and more filled out, came out to greet their relatives with traditional reserve.

"Come for a dooryard call, did ya?" smiled Perl.

Will, the elder and quieter of the two, disarranged the slicked-down hair on top of Robert's head and asked, "Want to see some baby kittens? New batch born just yesterday."

Robert and Frank followed along after Will to the barn.

"Come and set a spell," invited Perl. He gestured toward some old kitchen chairs sitting on the grass under a spreading white birch tree.

"So this is what you're driving these days, Stillman. How's that automobile do on these hills?" Perl or Will had never owned a motor vehicle.

Stillman answered the question. Then the discussion led to town politics, the Farmer's Almanac, and the changing of Woodstock now that city folk were buying up land.

"'Twon't be long before we git those electric lights just like over to Rutland and White River," Stillman commented.

"Wall, mebbe. But you won't be findin' any up here," Perl drawled. "Will and me, we do just fine without all them modern contraptions. Will holds the fort. I git down ta town for the necessaries and ta keep up on things, don't ya know."

Bessie could tell Stillman truly enjoyed time spent with her brothers. They were congenial, albeit unique.

After some time, Will came back with the boys and a half bushel of early apples. Bessie expressed her thanks and as Stillman began to get ready to leave, Will said, "If we had some ham, we could have ham and eggs – if we had some eggs!"

Bessie grinned at the familiar but halfhearted invitation to stay for a meal.

Stillman climbed into the passenger seat as he spoke. "Thanks for the offer, but no need. Gotta git back afore milkin'."

*   *   *

On the third of August, Frank came home from the woolen mill where he now worked. He had the *Vermont Standard* and the *Rutland Herald* under his arm. He handed the papers to Stillman before he washed up in the sink.

"What do you think of that?" he asked.

Stillman read the headlines with deliberate emphasis, "I DO NOT CHOOSE TO RUN. Well, I'll be! Ol' Cal's refusin' to go up for election next year. Sure throwin' in the towel early enough."

"Seems to me he's aged since he took on the presidency," added Bessie. "Takes a lot out of a man, I suspect."

"Things are going good. Hate to see a change right now. Guess he must have his reasons. No job I'd want. Hard enough to keep a farm goin'. Can't imagine runnin' the whull country."

* * *

October was wet and rainy. The rivers rose higher than usual. The leaves fell and rested on soggy ground.

But the hog was butchered, the apples picked and dried, and Mr. Copeland led his merino herd down off Long Hill and away to its winter quarters.

* * *

On Thursday, November third, Bessie and her family awoke to a thunderous sound.

"What's that noise?" Bessie shouted. In the dimness of early morning they could see rain pouring down outside. They heard the wind and the pelting of water against the window panes. And from the brook, roaring and crashing as they'd never heard before.

Stillman hurried into his clothes and ran outside. Shortly, he came back in to announce, "The dam's busted! Lumber's crashing downstream, banging into everything in

125

its path. Water's overflowin' the bank. Took our bridge with it. Log jams everywhere!"

For thirty-eight hours, the deluge kept up. Water converged from everywhere and ran through fields, gardens and buildings. Curtis Hollow Road looked like a river as water kept building and rushing downhill.

On Saturday, Stillman and other neighbors began to survey the damage to livestock, out buildings, crops and fences.

Open land had standing water. But the greatest adversity, it was discovered, was that Curtis Hollow had become isolated from Bridgewater. The swollen Ottaquechee had become a raging torrent and the force destroyed the bridge that connected the valley to civilization on the other side.

Each day as Stillman scouted the area, he would tell Bessie of the damage to other farms below and of huge logs he'd seen lying in woods and open fields far from their destination. Trees had been uprooted. The falls were reshaped as boulders in the brook had been pushed downstream. Debris was everywhere.

As farmers looked to their own repairs, they also lent a hand to their neighbors. Stillman expressed relief that there was only slight damage to his property. Those in lowland towns were hit hardest.

Soon, newspapers began reporting the effects of what was being called the 'Flood of 27'. Eighty-five Vermonters died, one of whom was Lieutenant Governor Jackson. Loss of livestock, railroads, bridges, roads, property and businesses was unparalleled. The paper reported nine thousand residents were left homeless throughout the state.

From the reports, Bessie found that although Vermont suffered the greatest losses, four other New England states were affected by the two severe storms that met over the northeast. She was deeply concerned about Alna, and it wasn't until four weeks later that she received a letter putting her mind at rest. All was well in Shrewsbury and Alna was still happy in her new life.

Tom Birmingham's men had a monumental task clearing the woods and the brook of logs and getting the operation back in order.

The wind bit at Bessie's face and stung her eyes as she stood at the backyard clothesline on a March afternoon. She tugged at the frozen pins to free stiff overalls. The imprints of the wooden clips remained on the pants like official seals of winter.

She brought the overalls inside and, like cardboard cutouts, draped them over the top of the parlor stove. As the heat began to penetrate, they molded to the shape of the stove and dripped until dry.

She felt a sharp pain in her back. Placing her hands on her hips, she straightened up and winced. That was the second hard pain that day. I must be getting old if I can't do a good day's work without hurting, she thought.

The men came in with their cold, wet boots and lined them up beneath the stove. The odor of heat on wet leather and woolen socks filled the room night after night.

"Will winter never end?" sighed Bessie.

It did. The cherry tree bloomed in late May. She spotted a brilliant Scarlet Tanager flitting from branch to branch. Then, a red-breasted robin, a red-headed woodpecker, a vibrant orange and black Baltimore Oriole, a tiny gold finch. The song birds brought joy to her heart. She listened to the tune each one sang. And if Robert was nearby, she would ask if he recognized the sounds. She wanted him to appreciate all of nature as she did, to take time to watch and listen.

*   *   *

Although life in the Hollow continued to run according to the season, news in the *Herald* told of massive reconstruction in the entire state. Over one thousand bridges had to be rebuilt. Miles of railway needed repair. Homes, roads, mills and numerous small businesses had to be restored. And Vermonters rose to the challenge.

*   *   *

In July on a Sunday, the Gays received company. Bessie was overjoyed to welcome Stillman's older sister, Mary, and her husband, Ralph Bowen. Bessie liked this couple. Mary was a gentle soft-spoken woman. Ralph, a carpenter, was talkative and jolly. He was reputed to be innovative in his use of wood and style of architecture. Bessie liked their home. It was nestled in the hills with a beautiful view of Little Ascutney Mountain. The interior of the house was light and airy with white birch woodwork throughout.

On this surprise visit, Ralph and Mary brought Bessie a present which was covered by a big towel. When Bessie peeked under the towel, she discovered a wire cage containing a soft lemon-colored canary. It began to chirp cheerfully as soon as the cage was uncovered. Bessie couldn't believe her eyes. She squealed with delight.

"I thought you'd like her," smiled Mary. "I told Ralph if ever there would be a good home for this bird, it would be with Bessie Gay! We're getting' just too old to care for another living thing. All's we can do to take care of ourselves. You remember our daughter, Minny, who was married to that Jones fella from Springfield? Well, now that he's gone, Minny and our granddaughter, Helen – would you believe she's nearly fourteen now and pretty as the morning sun – they upped and traipsed off to Springfield, Massachusetts! Just like your Alna goin' off so far. I swan', Bessie, what makes 'em leave like that?"

129

"Guess they need to see some of the outside world," Bessie ventured. "I s'pect V'mont will always be good enough for me."

"And the rest of the family don't stay put anymore, either," Mary continued as though Bessie had not spoken. "Well, yes, I s'pose these parts will keep us 'til we kick the bucket. Can't imagine livin' anywhere else, especially at our ages."

There was some catching up on news of the family. Mary talked about sister Alice and older brother, Hamden Hardy Gay. He had, as far as anyone knew, gone off to make his fortune in lumbering in New York State. No one had yet to hear from him, but each time the family came together, Hamden's name came up.

Then Stillman gave Ralph a verbal assessment of damage from the flood in the Hollow.

"When the bridge across the Ottaquechee at the mill washed out, the only way to cross was four miles down at Westerdale. That bridge was iron and didn't budge in the flooding. Frank had to walk the whull way down to pick up mail and supplies and then back track all the way back home. We were isolated from town for quite some time. Good deal of inconvenience, it was. We was all some happy when the mill bridge was rebuilt. Lucky, though. We didn't get much damage up here on the hill. Read in the papers about troubles down your way. How did you fare?"

Ralph told of devastation in their area and described the catastrophe in nearby Cavendish. "You wouldn't have believed your eyes. Folks came from miles around to see this gorge. I'm sure you read about it in the papers. Seems the Black River changed course and tore through Main Street cutting a hole six hundred feet long. And deep? You shoulda seen it! Anywheres from a hundred to four hundred feet in some spots. Like an earthquake had opened 'er up. Never seen nawthin' like it in my lifetime, I tell ya."

Bessie added, "When there's nothing else to talk about, folks can always tell tales about that flood. Nobody will ever forget it, I reckon. Something to be said for living on high ground. I feel sorry for those folks on the flats – White River Junction, Hartland, Barre, Rutland. Heard stories how some families with young ones were forced out of their places in the night with scarcely a place to go. Imagine! Nothin' but the clothes on their back and whatever they could carry."

"Bad business, a flood is. Pays no mind if you're rich or poor. Renders everyone the same troubles," Stillman sighed.

*   *   *

Frank and Stillman bought a 1925 Franklin touring car. It was sleek and black with an air-cooled engine. It was lightweight, economical, quiet, and Frank liked driving it.

Bert Curtis liked the looks of it so well he bought one for himself. One Saturday, Bert came chugging and jolting into the driveway. Frank was outside sawing some wood. Robert was chasing after his dog, Buster, and Bessie was carrying eggs from the coop.

Bert hopped out of the driver's seat. His face was red. He slammed the car door and kicked the front tire. "Judas Priest!" he exclaimed. "I'm turning this junk in! Hasn't run right since I bought it!"

Bessie watched Frank saunter over and lift the hood of Bert's car and poke around the engine.

"Looks all right," he offered. Start up the motor again."

Bert did as Frank suggested. "There! See what I mean? Won't start!"

"Wall, Bert, she's purrin' like a kitten. Can't ya hear 'er? That new self-starter shore is quiet."

Bert bent down closer. "Well, I'll be hung out ta dry! Durned if you ain't right. Must be my ol' ears ain't what they used to be. Guess I'll keep 'er after all. Much obliged."

*　　　*　　　*

That summer other relatives, the Baldwins from Springfield, came for a visit on a Sunday. Stillman decided to take them up to Ben Smith's place for some sweet cider. All the grown-ups left, but Robert and the Baldwin's son, Buster, remained at home with instructions from Frank to stay away from the Franklin. Bessie enjoyed the stimulating conversation as well as Ben's good cider.

The next morning, Frank took a long time getting the car started. Bessie heard him cranking and cranking with much frustration. Eventually he succeeded in getting the motor running. Mysteriously, all the switches had been turned on before morning. He told Bessie he couldn't figure out how it happened.

*　　　*　　　*

On July twenty-seven, Robert turned eleven. Stillman gave him eleven firm slaps on his bottom and one harder spank to 'grow on' as was the custom.

When the mail was brought home that afternoon, Frank was carrying a small package addressed to Robert. It was from Alna all the way from Massachusetts. Bessie saw the inquisitive delight on her son's face as he carefully opened the parcel. Inside was a boy's new white shirt and several folded pages of newspaper funnies.

"For pity sake," exclaimed Bessie. "A present on your birthday from your big sister. That shirt looks like it will fit fine and come in handy for the next Old Time Ball. All the girls will take notice; you can be sure!"

Robert reddened. "I like the funny papers!"

There was a letter for Bessie in the day's mail, also. As she read onto the second page of Alna's missive, her eyes grew large and her hand shook. She laughed out loud. Frank and Robert stared at her.

"What's she say, Mother? What's the matter?" asked Frank.

"You're going to be uncles, boys! And I'm going to be a grandmother come next April!"

"What do you mean, Mother?" asked Robert.

"Your sister is in the family way!"

"Wall, ain't that somethin'! declared Frank.

Robert marched off behind Frank and Bessie could hear his whispered voice. She was certain he had questions for Frank that were too delicate to ask one's mother.

The rest of the day Bessie nearly floated through her work. She sang to Happy the canary and Happy chirped back. She told Stillman the good news when he came in from the barn.

"A grandfather! Well, what do you know!"

"I think," said Bessie, "that I shall learn to drive the car. Then I could drive down next spring to help Alna. And I could go to church at times or get to town for necessities when you men are working. Yes, I believe that's what I'll do."

"I don't like the idea! Snapped Stillman. "Women driving cars. What next!"

Frank jumped to his mother's defense. "You could learn easy, Mother. Nawthin' to it. And it would be good to have another one to drive . . .." "He hesitated before going on, ". . . for emergencies and such."

"I'll have no more talk about this!" Stillman yelled.

Bessie knew the subject was closed, at least for now, and she gave Frank a look of caution which said proceed no further.

*   *   *

In the fall, Frank met a young lady at a South Pomfret dance. He told Bessie about her one night when Stillman was already abed.

She was a year younger than Frank. Her name was Teresa Mildred, daughter of Leon and Agnes Gray of the Taft farm on Westerdale Road, just above the Swanson farm. Mildred, as everyone called her, had been born in Morristown, New York. She was living in Woodstock where she did housekeeping for people on Elm and Pleasant streets. She attended St. James Episcopal Church at the head of the village green. Bessie knew that stately old church. It wasn't far from her sister Lora's house.

Frank said he thought she'd had a hard life at home and had been boarding out for some time, saving money and

134

helping her parents. He added that she seemed to know what she wanted in life.

"What does she look like?" asked Bessie.

Frank shrugged his shoulders. "Brown hair. Blue eyes, I guess. Seems taller than she really is."

"Do you like her?"

Frank nodded his head.

"Well," said Bessie, "if you like her, then so do I."

*   *   *

It was the kind of September day that gave hints of the harsh winter ahead but remained reluctant to let go of summer. Bessie wandered out to the field and waded through high corn with its rust-colored tassels reaching for the sky. She felt like a child again. How much taller the shocks were when she was young. Then, she would walk through row after row and pretend to be in her own private forest. Now, the stalks were scarcely taller than her height. But she still felt secluded and safe. She knew that soon the shocks would be cut down and tied up in sheaves leaving great bare spaces in this forest of corn. She plucked off an ear and ran her hand along the smooth silk. She held the silver green ear to her nose and inhaled the sweet fragrance. A good crop this year, she thought. She picked a few more ears, put them in her basket and headed reluctantly back to the house.

She glanced beyond to the hills. They resembled tapestry woven of shaded greens, tarnished gold and burnt orange with bits of magenta interspersed. But, she murmured to herself, the colors won't peak for another couple of weeks at least.

*   *   *

That week the *Herald* had a long article about President Coolidge traveling through Vermont by train. He had stopped to give a speech in Bennington. The paper covered the short speech about his beloved home state. Bessie read that he wanted to assess the flood damage and progress being made.

"Cal's term is prit' near over," Bessie commented as she laid the paper down. "Such a pity he isn't running again. Don't think I trust that Herbert Hoover. Having Cal in the White House is like having home folks run the country."

Stillman was nodding off. "Ayuh."

The following month Frank escorted Mildred to Felchville for a turkey supper and dance at the Reading Town Hall. Stillman went along, riding in the back seat of the Franklin.

On their second date, Frank took her again to a dance in South Pomfret. As usual, Stillman took the opportunity to go with the young couple and he also danced throughout the evening.

*   *   *

After a couple of hard frosts following Indian summer, the leaves peaked just as Bessie had predicted. Then snow came in late October, making her glad that Stillman and Frank had banked the house early in the month. And on

November fourth, the country elected fifty-four-year-old Herbert Hoover to the office of president over democrat candidate Alfred E. Smith. Bessie didn't vote.

* * *

November brought colorless days. Skies were grey. Trees were barren. Gone was the brilliance of maples and birches. Even the evergreens took on a grayish hue. The ground was a carpet of brown from dead leaves, mud and pine needles.

The weather grew cold and damp and the short days were busy with work to be completed before the real winter set in.

As Thanksgiving Day neared, Bessie suggested that Frank invite his friend, Mildred, for dinner. Frank said he would. Despite his impassiveness, Bessie knew he was smitten.

Thanksgiving Thursday dawned grey, cold and drizzly. There was a patchy layer of snow on the ground. Bessie missed Alna. It was her second Thanksgiving away from home. She wondered how she was feeling and if she was showing much. Letters back and forth were so slow.

She stuffed two large hens and put them in the oven. Then she set out peeling and cutting butternut squash and potatoes. All the time she talked to Happy and the bird tilted its lemony head as though it understood Bessie's concerns.

At a little past noon, Frank drove up with Mildred Gray. Bessie liked her immediately. She seemed sure of herself and started helping in the kitchen as soon as she arrived. Frank appeared pleased that Mildred and his mother were getting along so well. It pleased Bessie to have another woman in the kitchen.

Dinner went smoothly. Bessie offered a prayer of thanks. Stillman was reserved and quieter than usual. Bessie and Mildred kept up pleasant conversation about family and mutual acquaintances. Mildred talked about her sisters, especially the youngest, Marge. Frank and Robert were eating and listening, glancing at each other occasionally.

After the meal, when dishes were done, pies were eaten and cows were milked, the family retired to the parlor. The room was warm and cozy. Wood crackled in the stove. Nobody minded the wet, cold weather outside.

Mildred sat in the Morris chair. Robert knelt down behind where she was sitting and peeked around at her. Mildred laughed at his impish behavior.

Bessie sat down at her piano and began to play *Come Ye Thankful People, Come* and *Bringing in the Sheaves*. Then she continued with some of her favorite hymns—*The Old Rugged Cross, Blessed Assurance, He Leadeth Me,* and *In the Garden.*

Robert waited for a pause and said, "Mother, play that song about Charlotte, the lady who froze going to the dance 'cause she wouldn't wear a coat over her party dress."

Bessie smiled. "You like that, don't you, Bobby. Well, I'll play it if everyone will sing with me."

So Bessie played the ballad of *Poor Charlotte* while the rest joined her in singing the lyrics.

Then she played some lively Irish tunes. Frank and Robert kept time tapping their feet. Mildred clapped her hands. Stillman had his head thrown back on the settee and occasionally interjected loud snoring sounds into the festivities.

Too soon the day came to an end. Frank prepared to drive Mildred home. The rain had stopped and the moon was out, full, round and deep yellow. It illumined the remaining patches of frozen snow that glistened like diamonds. Bessie shivered as they stood on the porch. "Bundle up warm," she warned, "or you'll catch your death of cold!"

"Like Charlotte," Robert chimed in as Frank helped Mildred into the Franklin and tucked a blanket around her.

Mildred laughed. "But your brother is taking me home in a nice warm motor car, not a horse and buggy like her!"

A very tired Bessie collapsed into her bed where Stillman was already close to sleep.

*   *   *

Frank's third date with Mildred was on December thirteenth, her birthday. He took her to the dance in Plymouth along with their ever-present chaperone.

The following day, Frank told his mother that he had asked for Mildred's hand in marriage and she had accepted. Bessie was pleased. And pleased more so to see the excitement in the eyes of her undemonstrative son.

"Well, now that you'll be marryin' and movin' off the farm, I 'spect I'll have to learn to drive that automobile after all!"

Not that she would mention it, but Bessie was experiencing pain more frequently in her back and abdominal area. She seemed to be taking on weight in her midsection but she knew for a fact that she wasn't with child, and thankful for it at this point in her life. Sometimes the pain was so sharp she doubled over. At times, she became sick to her stomach and had very little appetite.

On her thirty-eighth birthday in January, she had knife-like pains between her shoulder blades and felt nauseous all day. She decided it must be more than just hard work. She determined to see Dr. Cram when she could find the time. With the lumbermen around, there was more to do and the weather didn't lend to traveling into Bridgewater just to see what ailed her. The winter days kept passing but not so her discomfort.

Frank was now escorting Mildred to church on Sundays. He was baptized and confirmed at St. James. Bessie was pleased even though the young lady of his life was the motivation for her son's sudden interest in things of the Spirit.

February was a frozen month. The cattle huddled in their stalls. Snow piled up against the sides of the house. Days were short and dark. Kerosene lamps worked overtime. The wood stoves burned hot. And Bessie was thankful for the one-pipe furnace in the cellar.

Bessie sat cracking and shelling butternuts and pondered over presidents she'd seen come and go. Then her mind wandered to her grandparents and all that they must have seen in their long lives. Her grandfathers, Isaiah Wheeler and Clark Stevens, were over eighty when they died. Bessie was a very young girl at that time and had a vague memory of seeing them once. Her grandmother, Julia

Wheeler, lived to be seventy-six and died the year Bessie was born, 1891. Her mother's mother, Margaret Stevens, was the only grandparent Bessie knew. She, too, lived past the age of eighty.

Bessie looked up from the pile of butternuts in her lap and gazed out the frosty window. No, she thought, I don't reckon I'd want to live in this world that long. Over forty more years of hard farm life and Stillman's intervals of brutality. And painful aging. It seemed more than she could bear to think about on this dreary March afternoon when it hurt even to sit up straight.

Bessie was able to see Dr. Cram in his office in Bridgewater toward the end of the month. He examined her after listening to her talk about the pain. He asked her how her life was going as he checked her heart and lungs with his stethoscope. He pressed on her stomach and she winced.

"Hurt right here, does it?" he asked sympathetically. When the examination was completed, he helped her sit up. He turned his back to write some notes on her chart while she hurriedly dressed. She let him know when it was prudent for him to turn around.

"Well, Miz Gay, it could be any number of things. You've led a hard life, farmin' and all. And two of those young 'uns you had put bad strain on your body big as they were, you know. I feel somethin' I 'spect is a growth in there, but we'll only know if we go in and take a look. Hard to tell with pain in the back like that. Could be all your heavy liftin' has taken its toll. Might be stones. Might not. I'm sendin' you over to Rutland Hospital as soon's I can make the arrangements. Dr. Ball will operate and see what's what. I'm suggestin' he do a hysterectomy. Not plannin' on havin' any more babies, are you?"

141

Bessie shook her head trying to take in all that her doctor was saying.

"Good. Then best take it all out so's you'll feel better. Don't you fret now. We'll have you fixed up in no time after some rest. You're a young woman with a lot of livin' to do. And you say you're goin' to be a grandma soon? Pshaw! Don't seem possible. And Frank. Plannin' on marryin', is he? I 'spect I'll be seein' him soon, then. Why, seems like no time ago 't all you delivered that scrawny little boy. Didn't think he'd make it, I tell you. Good to see what a fine, strappin' man he's turned out. You've got plenty of good reasons, then, to get rid of this pain and start feelin' better. I'll ring you up when I get a time for the operation. Try to slow down until then. Stillman's ribs still ailin' him? Bad fall, that was. Didn't help his arthritis ...or his moods, either, I 'spect. Give my regards."

Bessie mulled over the doctor's words for the next few days. The thought of surgery was frightening but she trusted Dr. Cram. And if he said she'd be feeling better, then that hope was stronger than her fear.

*   *   *

On March twenty-ninth, Frank presented Mildred with an engagement ring. The date they set for the wedding was April twentieth.

And the first part of April, Dr. Cram called to say Bessie's operation was scheduled for April thirteenth.

On Wednesday, April third, Bessie awoke with a sense of gloom. The sun was streaming through the back window. There were ice crystals shimmering on the bare branches. A promise of spring was forthcoming but she couldn't shake this strange oppression. She dressed quickly and went into the kitchen. Perfunctorily, she began preparing breakfast.

142

Frank ate hurriedly and left for the mill. Stillman gulped the last of his coffee and ushered Robert out to the barn for chores.

Only then did it occur to her. The kitchen was too quiet. She had forgotten to take the cover off her canary's cage.

As she lifted the cloth covering, she was horrified to see Happy laying on the bottom of his cage. She called to him and pleaded with him to wake up. But the canary was lifeless. Hot tears streamed down Bessie's face as she searched in the buttery for a small box with a lid. She carefully lifted the bird from its cage and wrapped it in the soft cloth that had protected it through the nights. Placing it tenderly in the box, she closed the lid and set the box on the table.

She went back to the duty of clearing dishes and straightening up the kitchen, crying softly all the while.

A short time later, Robert came in and looked alarmed when he saw his mother crying.

"Happy died in the night," she explained, wiping her eyes on her apron. "And before you go to school, I want you to dig a hole out back beneath the apple tree and bury him. He will be able to hear the wild birds sing back there."

Without saying a word, Robert carried the box outside while Bessie watched from the kitchen window. When Robert finished the task and came back inside, Bessie was still staring out the window softly singing *In the Shade of the Old Apple Tree*. She scarcely noticed as her son picked up his books and left for school.

143

If losing Happy caused profound sadness, the telephone call late on Saturday brought Bessie immeasurable joy. Nelson called from a hospital in Worchester to announce the birth of Richard Charles Swanson. Alna, he said, was doing well. She'd be in the hospital at least two weeks. Characteristically, Nelson imparted only necessary information and kept the conversation very short.

When Bessie set the ear piece back on the wall receiver, she twirled around the kitchen singing, "I'm a grandmother, I'm a grandmother!"

Then she began ringing up her sisters and her neighbors. She was so elated she couldn't stop herself from sharing the joyous news.

The next morning, she sat down early and wrote a letter to Alna telling her how proud of her she was and how happy the news of Richard Charles had made her. She assured her that they would drive down after the operation was over and the roads were safe to travel – perhaps in late May.

Bessie paused to dream about how exciting it would be to take such a long drive out of state and to see her daughter and new grandson. She wondered if the baby favored Alna or if he would have the slender, blond look of Nelson and his family. Oh, my, she thought. A Swedish baby in our family after such a long line of English ancestry. She smiled with great happiness.

She placed a stamp on Alna's letter and placed it on the little table near the front door. She'd remind Frank to mail it in town on his way to the mill in the morning.

On Monday there were snow flurries. She spent the better part of the day washing clothes, thankful the two boarders were gone and the loads were smaller. Her pain slowed her down and she was forced to rest for short intervals throughout the day.

Tuesday, after the men were out of the house, she heated up the flat iron on the stove and began pressing shirts and bed linens. She found she could lower her board and sit for most of the work.

That evening, she spent some time talking to Frank in the room he shared with his brother. She sat by Frank's bed and spoke in low tones that would not disturb her younger son's sleep.

Frank was concerned. "Mother, I believe Mildred and I should postpone the weddin' with you goin' in the hospital. I can have Mildred call the Reverend and set another day."

"You'll do no such thing, young man! That weddin' will go off as you've planned. You go ahead and get married. And when I get home we'll have the party and celebrate. And that's that. Now, tell me, are you plannin' to buy a new suit or shall I see what I can do with that brown wool of yours?"

Frank said the problem was all taken care of. He had already planned to borrow a blue suit from his friend at the mill.

"Good. Blue's a nice color. Suits your eyes, too."

As she got up from the chair, she glanced out the small window. "Spittin' snow again."

She tiptoed toward the stairs, past Robert's bed and she saw him shut his eyes quickly. Little rascal, she thought. He wasn't sleeping after all.

"Sleep tight, Bobby," she whispered in the moonlit room.

Wednesday dawned clear and crisp. Bessie set out a huge pan of dough to rise. Then she selected a large hen, killed and dressed it, and boiled it. By noon it was partially done. She drained some of the greasy broth from the kettle and added onions, carrots, potatoes, some flour and spices. She covered the pot and let the savory stew cook for two more hours.

In the meantime, she punched down her dough and shaped it into several loaves. By late afternoon, the aroma of baking bread filled the kitchen. She lifted the golden loaves from the oven just as Robert was coming in from school.

"Sit down, Bobby, and I'll slice you some bread with butter and sugar. Prit' near time to do the milkin' and lay some fresh hay. Your father's out fixin' fence by the John lot. Plenty stones to reset after this winter. Guess it's safe to take the banking off the house now, too. So much to do in spring. Like your father says, 'Life on the farm is all uphill living.' "

When she sat at her piano after supper she felt tired but satisfied that she had prepared some food ahead for Stillman and the boys. She knew Stillman would be able to manage making meals. When they ran the boardinghouse together, his biscuits and pies took a back seat to no one. Her men might not eat much variety, but there would be enough to fill their bellies while she was away.

She played some hymns to comfort her quaking heart. Tomorrow she would be in a strange place awaiting surgery on her body. She tried not to think about the fear that stalked her. As she played, she thought about her canary. How she missed hearing his cheerful chirping. She began singing and playing *In the Shade of the Old Apple Tree*. As much as she wanted to keep this day from ending, she was bone weary and needed rest. Perhaps after all this was over, she would begin to feel stronger. She began to pray but fell asleep in mid-sentence.

The family awoke to new fallen snow on Thursday. The white powdery flakes gave the farm a fresh, clean look. Bessie watched two mocha colored does trip gracefully down to the brook for their morning drink. They left a pattern of tiny hoof prints in the virgin snow. The deer stood out sharply against the background of white coated hills dotted with green. Bessie couldn't seem to take her eyes off them.

But there was work to do. She went upstairs into the storage area and found the old brown valise that had belonged to her mother. She dusted it off and placed in it her night dress, a few undergarments and her brushes. She supposed if she needed anything else, Stillman or Frank would bring it to her. She had no idea what she would need for a two-week stay in a hospital. She had never even been away from her home for overnight.

She set the valise by the front door and went outside to feed her chickens and rabbits. The hog was grunting, wanting to be fed, as well.

Stillman was chopping wood. She watched him as he swung the axe. She knew how hard it was for him to exert such energy. His arthritis was continually getting worse but he tried to keep going to manage the farm. Now with Frank leaving, he'd be losing a valuable hand. She didn't know how much longer he could keep up the pace that drove him. The fact that he was soon to be sixty-five was also a factor. She hoped he would not be hard on the boys while she was away. She felt she needed to be a buffer for them.

Inside, she dusted her piano and glanced up at the four portraits hanging on the wall above. They need dusting, too, she decided. She gazed at the picture of her husband when he was twenty-four years younger. What a handsome man I married, she thought. Tall, straight and healthy. So many years gone by, she whispered, as she looked at the youthfulness of her portrait. I was such a child. She dusted the glass and frames of the pictures of her two older children. Rosy cheeked little Alna and sweet Frank with his full little mouth and penetrating eyes. How she loved these portraits. Could these babies really be twenty and twenty-two already? She realized that there was no picture of Robert hanging there. And he's growing so fast, she thought. She purposed to think about getting a portrait of her youngest when she could arrange it.

By mid-afternoon, Frank came home from the mill. He stowed the valise in the back of the Franklin. Stillman came in and washed his hands and changed his shirt. Bessie took one more look around her house, and the three of them climbed into the car.

"Stop the car in front of the school, Frank," Bessie instructed. "I want to say goodbye to Bobby."

Frank pulled the car over and strode into the school house. He came out with his brother in step behind him.

Bessie opened the car door and leaned out. She threw her arms around her young son and kissed him.

"I'll see you in a while, Bobby. I'm going away to Rutland so I can get better. You'll always be a good boy, won't you?"

Robert nodded. He closed the door for her and they waved to each other. Then Robert scrambled back into the school building.

Bessie brushed away a tear and settled back for the long ride to Rutland.

She had to say goodbye to Frank and Stillman in the entrance room of the hospital. She hugged them both and kissed Frank on the cheek.

"Don't worry, Mother." Frank's voice started to crack as he tried to give her reassurance.

Stillman added, "Everything will be all right. We'll keep things runnin' 'til you get home. I'll be back on Saturday after your operation."

He patted her shoulder and brushed her forehead with his lips. And for a moment, Bessie was struck by his tenderness.

But, then, they were gone and apprehension seized her. She realized she was alone among strangers in a strange place.

*   *   *

The hospital was a stark, unfamiliar place with an antiseptic smell and busy people in crisp uniforms.

She was ushered into a large ward where small, high beds lined both sides of the walls. Most of them were occupied by women who were so enveloped in thin blankets

149

that they appeared to be wrinkled piles of linen. Some were death-like still. From others, came pitiful moans.

Attached to the foot of each bed was a wooden board displaying the patient's chart. There was a sink in one corner of the austere room. Near the door there was a desk where a stern, bespeckled nurse sat writing in a record book.

Bessie's attention was drawn to the electric bulbs which gave the room its dim light. There were no kerosene lamps to be seen. And no familiar coal oil smell.

What arrested her sense of smell was the acrid odor of urine mingled with strong disinfectants.

She was instructed to undress and get into one of the empty beds.

*   *   *

For the remainder of that day and the next, hospital attendants came and left. They asked her questions over and over. They examined her, probed her stomach, took her temperature, and used their cold stethoscopes on her chest and back. She was given foul tasting medicine and offered clear broth and tea, but she scarcely touched the food. She had no appetite.

As the day passed into night on Friday, she heard nurses talking about the snow falling outside.

"Comin' down hard 'n fast," they reported to each other. "No tellin' how much'll fall before mornin'. We're likely to be stranded here!"

That news gave Bessie something else to be concerned about. She stared at the ceiling and tried not to hear the sounds of painful sobbing in the darkened room. She concentrated on home and wondered how much snow was falling there. She hoped Stillman wouldn't try to make the trip to Rutland if the weather was bad. She didn't want Frank taking chances with the Franklin for such a hard ride. She wanted to think of her family warm and safe inside sitting in the parlor after a hearty supper of her chicken stew and buttered bread.

She longed to look outside to watch the snow but there were no windows. And the medicine that she had just been given was beginning to make her drowsy.

Bessie lay on the cold operating table, stilled by the strangeness of the sterile room. Only her eyes moved from side to side, watching the nurse and the doctor as they prepared to work on her. There was no softness about the nurse as she darted back and forth in her starched white uniform. Doctor Ball spoke in a low voice to the nurse in conversation that Bessie could not understand. How she longed for a familiar face, a soothing word. If only Dr. Cram could have been there.

She forced herself to think of other matters. She tried to envision Alna's week-old baby, Richard—his eyes, his cheeks, his tiny fingers. In the summer she would see him. It wouldn't be so long, she comforted herself.

She thought about Frank and Mildred and their wedding next week. Even though she knew she couldn't attend the ceremony, she looked forward to the party at the house as soon as she was well enough. She'd miss Frank not living in the house. He was her strong, quiet soldier. Her protector and confidant. How would she manage Stillman in his bad times without Frank?

And she thought about Robert. Such a big boy but worked too hard for his eleven years. She knew he was dependent upon her and feared his father. If only Bobby could have known Stillman in his younger days before the pain and hard drinking began. If he could have known more of his sense of humor and the reasons she had admired him so. She vowed to have a talk with Bobby when she returned home and tell him about good times.

Suddenly, something black was cupped over her nose and mouth.

"Don't fight the ether. Just breathe deeply," the impassive nurse ordered.

Bessie wanted to grab the black contraption and pull it off her face, but she was helpless. Her hands and legs were strapped down, and she felt oppressed by an invisible weight.

The room began to spin. She closed her eyes. She heard the doctor's voice reverberating like an echo. She saw her old home in East Barnard. She saw Lime Pond and the surrounding mountains. Sounds were echoing across the valley. They were the voices of Will and Perl, Lora and Lottie. She saw her mother's face vividly silhouetted against a grey sky. There were black and white piano keys before her. Her fingers touched the keys and all the notes echoed across the mountain valley.

Faster and faster the notes played. She felt she was plummeting into a dark place. The mountains turned black. There was no moonlight. No fear. Only silence.

Suddenly, there was light! Light so dazzling that for an instant she didn't see the Hand that was reaching out to her or hear the Voice that called her name.

"Bessie!"

Epilogue

It snowed two more feet on the night of April twelfth. On Saturday morning, Stillman was determined to get to Rutland to see his wife, but the road over the mountain was closed. He hitched up the oxen and sleigh and had Frank drive him to the depot in Woodstock.

He boarded a train to White River Junction and rode down to Bellows Falls. From there, he transferred to a northbound train to Rutland.

When he finally arrived at the hospital, chilled and exhausted, he learned that Bessie had died at two-thirty that afternoon. He was two hours too late. Dr. Ball explained that she didn't survive the operation. Through a haze of disbelief, Stillman heard him say something about the shock of surgery to her system.

*   *   *

In the afternoon, Frank and Robert trudged through the snow down to Bridgewater to get the mail and a few groceries. On the way home, Marcia Curtis called to the boys from her front porch. She told them she'd received a call from Stillman in Rutland. Their mother was gone and their father wouldn't be home that night.

Frank and Robert walked the rest of the way home and entered the dark, quiet house without saying a word. The groceries sat in the bags on the table next to the mail which remained unopened.

*   *   *

They laid Bessie to rest in Quechee on the hill above Dewey's Mill in a grave near her mother on Stillman's plot.

They placed a small, insignificant stone marker there which simply read:

Bessie M. Wheeler, wife of S. O. Gay

But it didn't matter. Quechee was not her home. She had a place prepared for her in her Father's House.

And the angels rejoiced at Bessie's homecoming.

Author's Notes

1. Bessie Maude Wheeler died at age 38 on Saturday, April thirteenth, 1929 during surgery on her appendix, gall bladder and a hysterectomy. Her death was called surgical shock.

2. Frank and Mildred were married quietly on the following Saturday, April twentieth. They had a sixty-six-year marriage until Frank's death in 1995. Mildred continued to reside in Woodstock until her death at 104 years of age.

3. The house and barns in Curtis Hollow burned to the ground in Early November of 1930.

4. Alden Wheeler died November eighth, 1930 in Hanover hospital. He is buried in Quechee with his wife, Clara.

5. A violin made in prison by Calvin Coolidge's cousin was given to Robert. He sold it to an Italian boarder in his Uncle Idey's home for twenty-five dollars and another violin. The trade violin was the one on which Robert learned to play.

6. Robert <u>did</u> slide past Curtis Hollow School one day and had to walk all the way back up the hill.

7. Stillman and Robert went to live with Frank and Mildred on a farm in the Cox district of Woodstock in 1931. They had lived with neighbors until that time. Stillman grew progressively more difficult, crippled and helpless.

8. Calvin Coolidge died on January fifth, 1933 at age sixty and was buried in Plymouth, VT.

9. Stillman died on Bessie's birthday, January twenty-third, 1933. He, too, is buried in Quechee.

10. Robert joined the Civilian Conservation Corps in the summer of 1933, working in road construction and various improvement projects around the state of Vermont.

11. Robert married Ivis Lucille Woodley of Hartland on November twenty-second, 1936 in Woodstock. She was the daughter of George Woodley and Grace Maud Bohonon.

12. Bert Curtis developed a type of periodontal disease and died in Rutland Hospital around 1936.

13. Alna and Nelson moved back to Bridgewater in 1941 and lived on the farm Nelson's parents had owned. Nelson died in 1963 and Alna eventually moved to Springfield where she lived until her death in 1995.

14. Perly Wheeler became a renowned figure in Woodstock. His photographs were on greeting cards and in the New York World's Fair. He was visited by Lowell Thomas, written about in periodicals, and interviewed by the BBC that dubbed him the Duke of Breezy Heights. Perly and his brother, Will, are buried side by side in the River Street Cemetery in Woodstock.

15. Robert and his family moved to Connecticut in 1954. Robert subsequently moved to Florida where he lived until his death in 1996.

Robert – Early 1970's

Bessie's Children: Alna, Robert, Frank – 1970's

Perly Wheeler

Alna and Mildred, Sisters-in-law

The Old Place

The cellar hole remains there still, and few are those who know
The secret of its hiding place beneath the weeds that grow.

What memories are hidden there. What stories it could tell
Of boys who walked the hill for cows and fished the brook as well;

Of Grandma's man who went to fight the Civil War, and died
Leaving a son he never knew to farm the land with pride;

A Mom who raised her family with all the love she knew;
A Dad who worked in spite of pain 'til each hard day was through;

Hoeing fields and planting seed, wading through high corn;
Boys who skied their way to school on many a snowy morn;

White-tail in the mowing, wood stacked near the door,
Sugar-on-snow and Johnny cake, and canning jars in store;

Hymns and Irish melodies sung on a winter's eve;
Lumbermen who boarded there and stories they would weave;

Times to learn and times to grow in heartache, joy and tears;
A home that was provider and protector through the years.

Oh, God, in Your eternal plan, when change must come at last,
Preserve that little cellar hole and memories of its past.

Donna D'Addario
1985

159

GAY - WHEELER ANCESTRY

Andrew Stevens and Marcy Collins
1731-1808   1734-1804

Rev. Andrew Stevens and Sarah Clark
1765-1840   1770

Nathaniel Stevens and Elizabeth Chamberlin
1789-1860   1778-

Clark Stevens and Margaret Manning
1815-1897   1825-1906

Isaiah Wheeler and Julia Foster
1816-1899   1815-1891

Clara B. Stevens and Alden Wheeler
1854-1917   1855-1930

Lora   Will   Lottie   Perly
1878-   1879-   1881-   1881-1966
          1959   1962

Artar and Hannah Rogers

Richard Gay and Lucy Rogers
1798-1853   1803-1862

Stillman O. Gay and Roana Emmons 1840-1912
1836-1864   (m. Will. Dugan)
                   1842-1934

Stillman Orvis Gay ——— m. 1905 ——— Bessie Maude Wheeler
1864-1933   1891-1929

160

DIRECT DESCENDANTS OF STILLMAN and BESSIE GAY

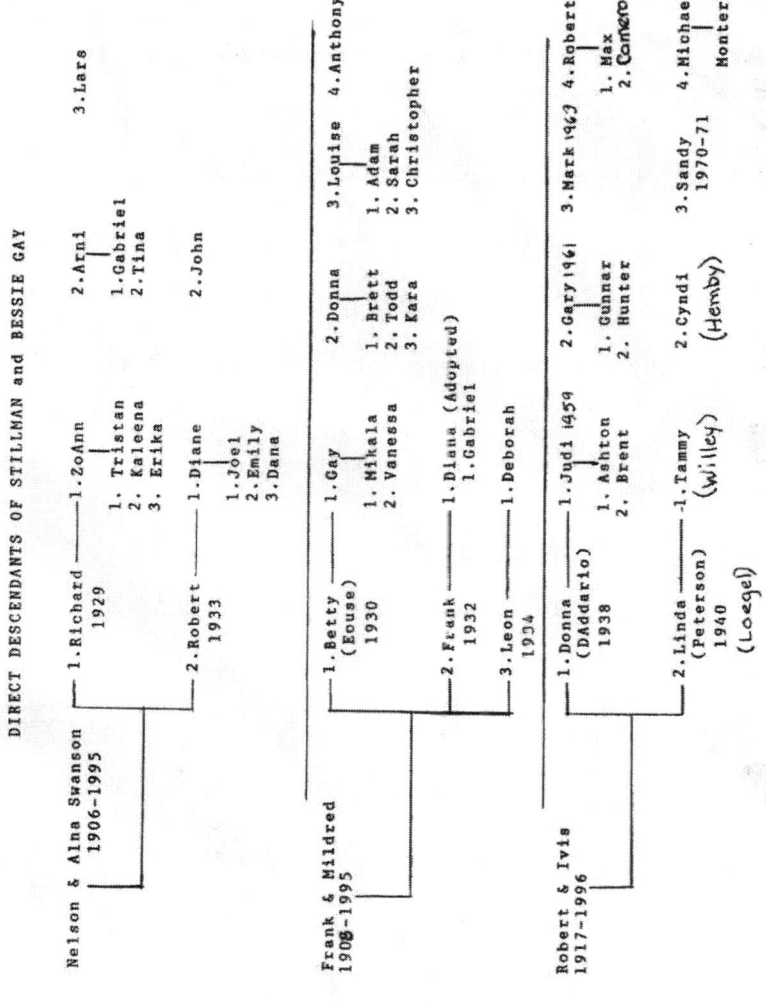

Nelson & Alma Swanson
1906-1995

- 1.Richard 1929 —— 1.ZoAnn   2.Arni   3.Lars
    - 1. Tristan
    - 2. Kaleena
    - 3. Erika
    - 1.Gabriel
    - 2.Tina
- 2.Robert 1933 —— 1.Diane   2.John
    - 1.Joel
    - 2.Emily
    - 3.Dana

Frank & Mildred
1908-1995

- 1.Betty (Eouse) 1930 —— 1.Gay   2.Donna   3.Louise   4.Anthony
    - 1.Mikala
    - 2.Vanessa
    - 1. Brett
    - 2. Todd
    - 3. Kara
    - 1. Adam
    - 2. Sarah
    - 3. Christopher
- 2.Frank 1932 —— 1.Diana (Adopted)   1.Gabriel
- 3.Leon 1934 —— 1.Deborah

Robert & Ivis
1917-1996

- 1.Donna (DAddario) 1938 —— 1.Judi 1959   2.Gary 1961   3.Mark 1963   4.Robert 1969
    - 1. Ashton
    - 2. Brent
    - 1. Gunnar
    - 2. Hunter
    - 1. Max
    - 2. Cameron
- 2.Linda (Peterson) 1940 (Loegel) —— 1.Tammy (Willey)   2.Cyndi (Hemby)   3.Sandy 1970-71   4.Michael Monterey

Bibliography

An Album of Hartford Vermont, date 7, pp. 206-213

Bicentennial Vermonter 1791-1991, Vergennes, Douglas Lazarus

Bridgewater Mill Mall Pamphlet, Bridgewater, VT, History

Calvin Coolidge The Quiet President, Donald McCoy, Macmillan Co., NY 1967

Cars of the Early Twenties, Tad Burness, Chilton Book Co., Philadelphia, 1968, pp. 112-115

Ford 1903-1984, Lewis, McCarville, Sorensen, Publications International Ltd., 1983,
p. 79

Grace Coolidge and Her Era, Isabel Rose, Dodd, Mead & Co., NY, 1962, p. 172

Herbert Hoover, A Biography, Eugene Lyons, Doubleday & Co., 1964, p. 184

Historical Highlights of Hartford, VT, 1974, pp. 336-343

History of Hartford, 1888, pp. 117-120

History of Barnard, VT, Vol. 11, pp. 126, 340-382, W. M. Newton, 1927

Pictorial History of American Presidents, John and Alice Durant, Barnes & Co., N.Y., 1955

Return to These Hills, Jane and Will Curtis and Frank Lieberman, Curtis Lieberman Books, Woodstock, 1985 Yankee Bookshop

Revised Roster of VT Volunteers and lists of VTers who served in the Army and Navy of the U. S. During the War of the Rebellion, 1861-1866, Montpelier, 1892

The American Automobile, Ralph Stein, Ridge Press Book, Random House, NY

Vermont Life, Spring 1991, p. 19, "Young Charlotte"

Vermont Life, Fall 1997, p. 4, "Great November Deluge," 1927
Vermont Life, Winter 1990, pp. 3-11, "Turning Points"

Vermont Standard, Feb., 1995, Vol. 141, No. 33, p. 2, Gold Hunters

Volume Library 1 and 2, Southwestern Co., Nashville, 1986

Yankees Remember, Yankee, Inc., Dublin, NH, 1st Edition, 1976

Other Sources

Alna Swanson, personal letters

Bessie M. W. Gay, poem found in daughter Alna's Bible

Cemeteries in Woodstock, W. Woodstock, Quechee, Bridgewater

Orella Woodley Colburn, research

Retracing the land of Curtis Hollow, E. Barnard, Quechee at Dewey's Mills, Bridgewater Woolen Mill, Woodstock and other outlying areas.

Richard Swanson, genealogy research

Robert O. Gay, his stories, poems, maps, diagrams, theories, and conversations

Theresa Mildred Gay, personal letters and conversations

Town Clerks of Reading, Hartford, Hartland, Woodstock, and Barnard, VT

"Up Hill Living," Alna Swanson, Memoirs

About the Author

Donna Gay D'Addario is the granddaughter of Bessie Wheeler Gay. She lives in Fairfield, CT with her husband Joseph. They have four children, six grandchildren, and one great grandchild.

It is her desire that those who read this story be inspired by Bessie's life.

Made in the USA
Middletown, DE
19 September 2016

HURRAY

by Jer

CONTENTS

ROURKE CLASSROOM RESOURCES
The path to student success

What Are Plants?

Plants are living things that don't move on their own. They grow on land or in water.

Kelp and algae are plants that live in the ocean. There are forests of kelp, just as there are forests of trees on land.

Green plants can
make their own food.
They make their own
food from water and
sunlight.

Plants are made up
of cells with very stiff
walls. You need a
microscope to
see them.

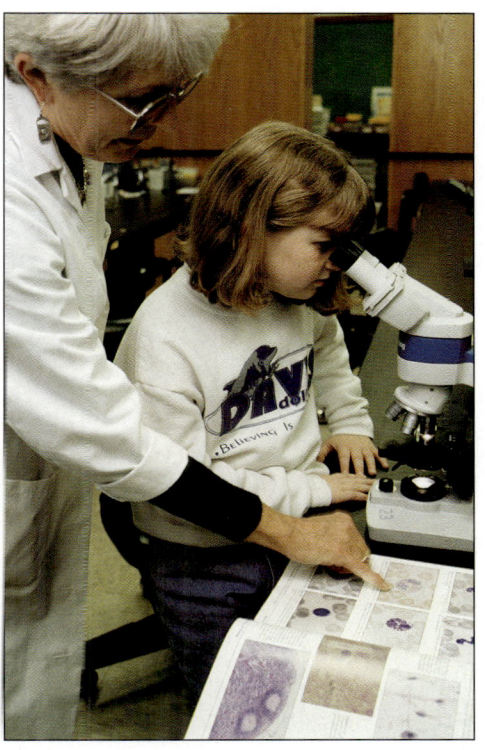

Are These Plants?

Fungi, such as mushrooms and toadstools, look like plants. Scientists used to think they were plants, but now they do not. Fungi are different than plants.

Fungi do not have green leaves. They cannot make their own food. They get their food from decaying or living plants.

How Do Plants Make Food?

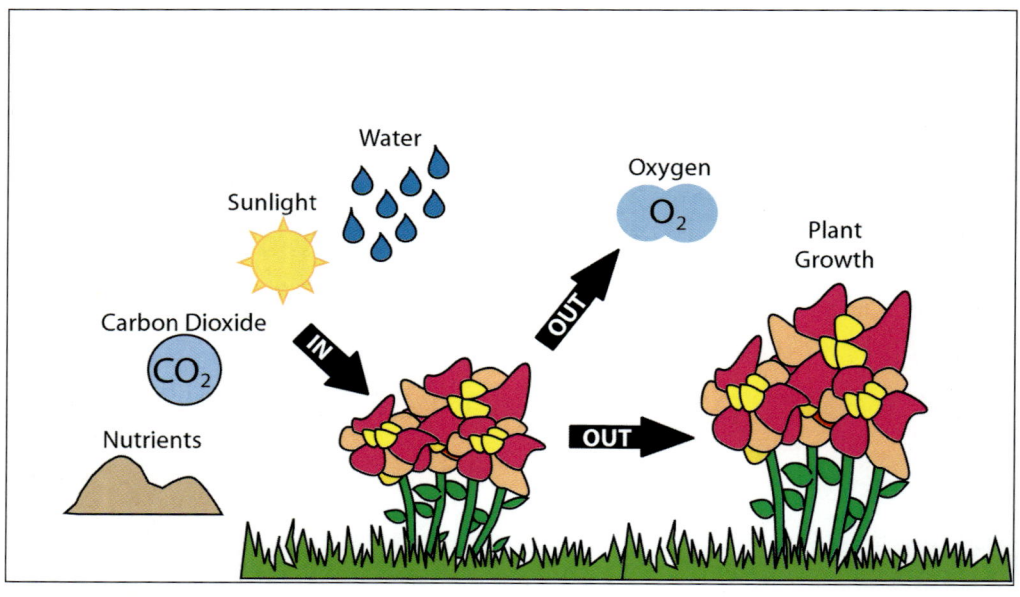

Green plants make food through a process called photosynthesis.

A plant's leaves are like little factories. Green chloroplasts in the leaves take in light **energy** from the sun.

Water comes up to the leaves from the plant's roots. A gas called **carbon dioxide** (CO_2) comes in through **stomata**, or tiny holes in the leaf. The plant uses water and CO_2 to produce sugar and **oxygen**.

Who Needs Plants?

People and animals need plants. Without plants we could not live! People and animals cannot make their own food. Plants make food and

store energy. People and animals eat plants to get energy.

There may be as many as 260,000 types of plants in the world.

Oxygen From Plants

Plants give us oxygen, too. Without plants, people and animals could not live! We need to breathe oxygen (O_2). Plants make that oxygen. Oxygen helps us turn the food we eat into energy.

Running takes oxygen.

Buffalo are herbivores—plant eaters.

During the day, plants give off oxygen as they make food. The oxygen goes out the leaf stomata and into the air around us. Lucky for us that they give off more oxygen than they use themselves.

All of the oxygen in the air comes from plants. Earth's atmosphere is 20% oxygen, 79 % nitrogen, 1% other gasses including carbon dioxide.

Plants Need Us Too

Day and night, our bodies burn the fuel that comes from eating food. As we burn fuel, we breathe out carbon dioxide (CO_2). The CO_2 goes into the air. Plants take in the CO_2. They use it to make food and oxygen. The whole process repeats over and over and over.

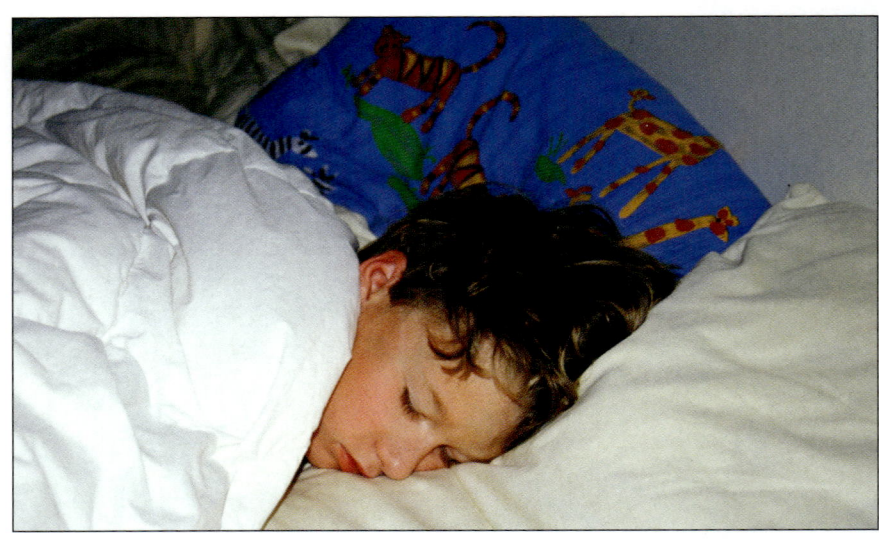

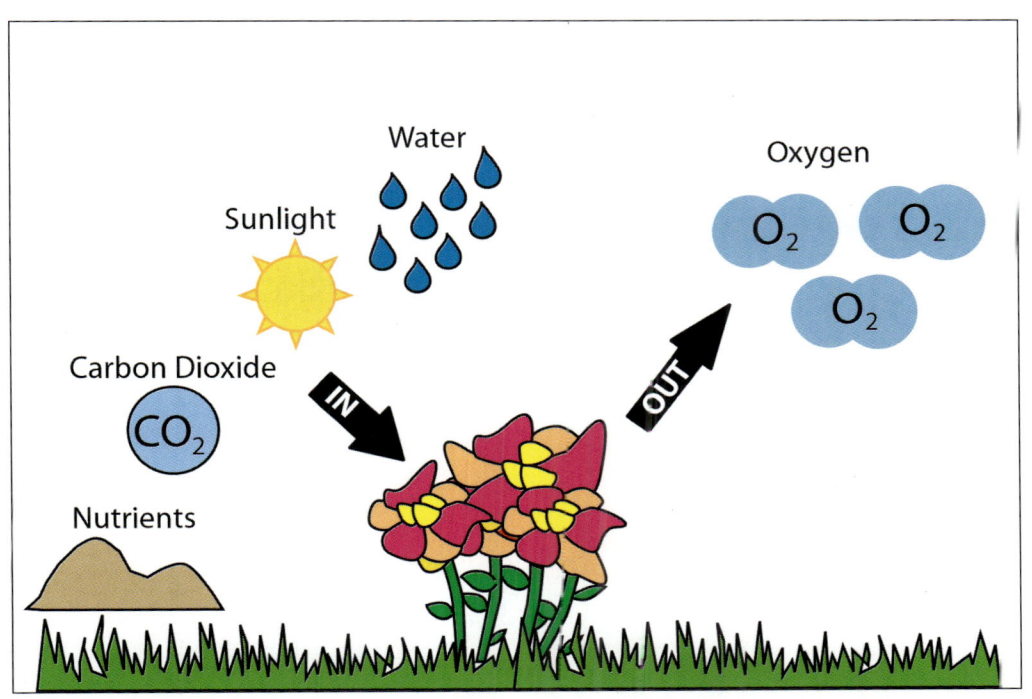

13

Plant Superheroes

Some plants can help clean the **pollution** in our air. Their leaves trap harmful **fumes** and chemicals. We plant Gingko and poplar trees on city streets to clean the air.

The food we eat and the oxygen we breathe comes from plants. So, take a deep breath and thank a plant!

GLOSSARY

carbon dioxide   a colorless gas made from carbon and oxygen

energy   power to move and grow

fumes   smoke or vapors, usually smelly

fungi   living plant-like things that do not get food from photosynthesis

oxygen   a colorless gas that people must breathe in order to live

pollution   fumes or other wastes that can harm the air we breathe or the water we drink

stomata   tiny openings or pores in plant leaves

INDEX